BOLD BUT CAUTIOUS

BOLD BUT CAUTIOUS

Balancing Legal Risks with Business Strategies

JOHN C. VESCERA

atmosphere press

LEGAL DISCLAIMER

The information provided in this book is for general information purposes only, should not be taken as legal advice, and does not purport to be a substitute for the advice of legal counsel on any specific matter. There is no attorney-client relationship created by this book. For legal advice, you should consult with legal counsel concerning your specific situation.

ABOUT THE AUTHOR

JOHN C. VESCERA is a California lawyer providing solutions-driven legal representation to privately held and publicly traded companies operating in highly regulated, highly competitive industries subject to state and federal consumer protection laws. John has worked with national and international companies, bringing strategic solutions to complex legal matters and helping clients balance legal risks with business strategies. He has authored the books *Chasing Corporate Compliance* and *Bold But Cautious.*

ACKNOWLEDGMENTS

To my clients who have encountered unique and multifaceted legal issues, thank you for inspiring this book.

To my wife, Kathy, thank you for your support in my writing this book, welcomed suggestions, creative cover design, and contribution of your outstanding editing skills.

CONTENTS

CHAPTER 4 73
LEGAL RISK MITIGATION STRATEGY

Prologue

In life, being bold but cautious is a worthy approach to achieving personal objectives. It combines the willingness to take risks and pursue opportunities with a thoughtful and measured mindset.

In business, being bold but cautious is an important proactive approach for balancing legal risks with business strategies. It involves integrating legal considerations into the decision-making process to ensure that business objectives are pursued within the boundaries of applicable laws and regulations while innovating and growing the business.

Bold But Cautious presents the delicate balancing act between legal risks and business strategies. On the one hand, businesses need to take risks to innovate and grow. On the other hand, businesses need to be aware of the legal risks involved in their activities and take steps to mitigate those risks.

Being bold doesn't mean being reckless. By carefully considering the legal risks, conducting thorough research, and implementing strategic safeguards, innovative and daring business strategies can be pursued. Being bold but cautious is about finding the right balance between courage and prudence!

Bold But Cautious is written from a compendium of experiences, insights, and hard-earned wisdom garnered from the frontlines of both law and business and explores the symbiotic relationship between legal expertise and entrepreneurial innovation.

As the ink meets the page, it is with the earnest hope that this book will serve as a guide for seasoned lawyers thriving in the global marketplace where legal acumen is inseparable from entrepreneurial vision, for the courageous business founder seeking to unlock the mysteries of the legal labyrinth and regulatory landscape, for fresh legal minds embarking upon the corridors of the legal profession, and for those poised on the precipice of a new professional journey where the intersection of law and business defines the prospect of achievement.

CHAPTER 1
Balancing Legal Risks with Business Strategies

Balancing legal risks with business strategies is a critical aspect of corporate governance. It involves integrating legal considerations into the decision-making process to ensure that business objectives are pursued within the boundaries of applicable laws and regulations, as well as other legal risk factors. By integrating legal considerations into strategic decision-making, businesses can proactively manage risks, protect their reputation, and create a solid foundation for sustainable growth. Legal guidance should not be an afterthought but an integral part of the strategic decision-making process from the very beginning to contribute to long-term success.

Role of Legal Counsel

Legal representation plays a crucial role in the corporate context, helping businesses navigate a complex web of laws, regulations, and legal issues. Whether it's a small startup or a multinational corporation, legal representation serves various essential functions.

Lawyers advising companies or acting as in-house counsel need to have a solid understanding of both the business and the industry in which the company operates so they can effectively mitigate legal risks, as well as adequately communicate with business stakeholders and senior management. A lawyer who lacks an understanding of the business operations or the rudiments of the business strategy is far less able to develop fundamental risk mitigation strategies or work with the non-lawyer management teams to consider ways of safeguarding the organization with business goals in mind.

Lawyers advising companies must demonstrate knowledge of the company's business fundamentals so they can educate and guide stakeholders on relevant issues and trends, speaking in value-based language instead of legalese among non-lawyers.

Lawyers can improve their advisory assessments by using data analytics to enhance and support their suggested solutions to mitigate legal risks and drive a risk mitigation culture in day-to-day operations.

Balancing legal risks with company business strategies involves understanding the legal landscape and integrating risk management practices into business operations. Some key points:

- **Understand the Business Goals:** Lawyers need a deep understanding of the company's business goals and strategies. This includes knowing the company's industry, target market, growth plans, and financial objectives. This understanding helps lawyers align their legal advice with the company's overall mission.

- **Legal Context:** Laws and regulations can vary significantly from one industry to another. A lawyer who understands the industry can better navigate the specific legal challenges and compliance issues that the company might face.

- **Tailored Advice:** Every industry has its unique set of challenges, risks, and opportunities. Lawyers who understand the business model and specific industry can provide tailored legal advice that takes these factors into account.

- **Effective Communication:** Understanding industry-specific terminology, trends, and practices helps lawyers communicate more effectively with their client's management teams to ensure that legal considerations are integrated into various projects and aspects of the business strategy. Legal advice must be clear, relevant, and easily understood by the business stakeholders so that business decisions are formed with legal considerations.

- **Strategic Counsel:** A lawyer who knows the business and industry can provide strategic advice that aligns with the company's goals. They can anticipate legal issues that might arise and help the company develop proactive strategies to mitigate risks.

- **Alternative Approaches:** Lawyers who possess a thorough knowledge of the industry, regulatory environment, and business objectives can suggest alternative solutions to operations and certain processes, such as marketing strategies to mitigate legal risks or opening new markets with the proper legal safeguards.

- **Contractual Matters:** Many legal matters involve contracts. Having a grasp of the industry helps lawyers draft contracts that are specific to the industry's needs, ensuring that all relevant considerations are addressed.

- **Legal Precedents:** Lawyers having a working understanding of the industry and business can effectively research legal precedents, regulations, and industry standards relevant to the proposed business strategy. This information is essential in providing meaningful advice on how the strategy might align or conflict with existing legal requirements. The legal landscape and business environment are constantly evolving.

Staying updated on industry news, new laws, applicable legal case decisions, regulations, and industry trends is key to providing timely and relevant advice.

- **Regulatory Compliance:** Industries are subject to various regulations and standards. A lawyer who understands the industry can help the company stay compliant with these regulations, avoiding costly penalties and legal disputes.

- **Legal Risk Management:** Every business operates within a legal framework that includes regulations, contracts, intellectual property rights, labor laws, and more. Identifying and managing legal risks requires an understanding of both the legal landscape and the industry context. Lawyers who are well-versed in both areas can create comprehensive risk management strategies.

- **Efficient Problem-Solving:** Lawyers who understand the company's business and industry can quickly identify legal issues and devise practical solutions. This efficiency saves time and resources for the company.

- **Building Trust:** Developing a strong lawyer-client relationship or strong in-house counsel-stakeholder relationship relies on trust. Clients/stakeholders are more likely to trust lawyers who demonstrate a deep understanding of their business and industry.

- **Negotiations and Disputes:** In negotiations and disputes, knowing the industry's norms and practices can be advantageous. Lawyers can better represent the organization's interests by leveraging this knowledge.

- **Flexibility and Agility:** Aligning and balancing legal risks with business strategies enhances a company's ability to respond quickly to legal challenges and opportunities. It allows for agile decision-making in situations that require prompt action to advance business goals while mitigating legal risks in rapidly changing business environments.

- **Scenario Planning:** Lawyers well-informed about the industry and business can work with business teams to develop various scenarios, considering how legal risks might play out under different circumstances. This enables the company to be prepared to respond swiftly if a legal challenge arises.

- **Training and Education:** Regular training sessions for the business teams can help improve mutual understanding. Business teams can learn about basic legal concepts, while lawyers can gain insights into the organization's operational realities.

- **Ethical Considerations:** Lawyers should always uphold their ethical responsibilities, which might involve advising against a business strategy that poses substantial legal risks or a business strategy that may have ethical concerns or complications. The key is finding ways to align business objectives with legal and ethical principles.

In essence, the intersection of legal expertise and industry knowledge is where effective corporate legal counsel thrives. This combination allows lawyers to provide valuable guidance that not only addresses legal concerns but also contributes to the company's overall success.

Balancing legal risks with business strategies requires a delicate equilibrium between legal expertise and business acumen. It's an ongoing process that requires proactive collaboration and adaptability to achieve both legal compliance and business success.

In summary, legal representation is integral to the corporate world, providing essential guidance and support to companies across a wide range of legal and business matters. Legal experts assist companies to operate within the bounds of the law while supporting business growth and protecting their interests.

Legal Counsel's Balancing Act: Risk versus Reward

Is the risk worth the reward? Attorneys and business leaders wrestle with this critical question as they consider a variety of business decisions related to new products or services, new markets, and partnering with third parties. Corporate counsel often find themselves engaged in a delicate balancing act between legal risk and organizational reward. Their role involves providing legal advice and guidance to company decision-makers while considering the potential legal risks and benefits associated with various actions.

Weighing legal risk and innovation requires legal counsel to keep pace with changes throughout the organization, including pivots in strategic priorities, with a variety of stakeholders. Often, business teams do not appreciate how even the slightest difference in business strategy can result in increased legal risk outcomes.

It is important that legal counsel be given enough time to evaluate the potential impacts of a developing product or business strategy to analyze whether the benefits are worth the legal risk or if the business strategy requires adjustment accordingly. Here's a closer look at this balancing act:

- **Legal Compliance versus Business Objectives:** Corporate counsel need to ensure that the company's actions are compliant with applicable laws and regulations. However, they must also consider the company's strategic goals and business objectives so as not to stifle business growth. Balancing these two aspects involves finding ways to achieve business goals while staying within legal boundaries.

- **Risk Mitigation versus Innovation:** While avoiding legal risks is crucial, overly cautious advice can hinder the company's growth and ability to innovate and take calculated risks. Corporate counsel need to assess the potential legal risks of new initiatives against the potential rewards they can bring to the company.

- **Preventive Measures versus Reactive Responses:** A strategic corporate counsel not only addresses legal issues as they arise but must also implement preventive measures to minimize the occurrence of legal problems. Striking a balance between proactive legal mitigation efforts and reactive responses to immediate legal challenges is essential.

- **Transparent Communication versus Confidentiality:** Corporate counsel need to maintain open lines of communication with company stakeholders while safeguarding sensitive legal information. Balancing transparent communication with the need to maintain attorney-client privilege is vital to maintaining trust and legal protection.

- **Short-Term versus Long-Term Perspectives:** Some legal decisions may yield immediate benefits but could have negative long-term legal consequences. Corporate counsel must consider the long-term impact of their advice and actions on the company's reputation, legal standing, and sustainability.

- **Legal Certainty versus Ambiguity:** Legal issues often come with a degree of uncertainty. Corporate counsel must provide guidance even when the law is not entirely clear, balancing the need for decisive action with the potential risks associated with unclear legal terrain.

- **Balancing Expectations:** Balancing the expectations of various stakeholders, including executives, employees, shareholders, regulators, and the public, can be challenging. Corporate counsel must consider the diverse interests and perspectives while making legal recommendations, however, in the best interests of safeguarding the organization.

- **Ethical Considerations:** Corporate counsel have a duty to act ethically and in the best interests of their clients. Balancing ethical considerations with legal requirements and business objectives is a fundamental aspect of the role.

- **Adaptation to the Changing Legal Landscape:** Laws and regulations evolve over time. Corporate counsel need to stay updated on legal changes and adapt their advice accordingly to ensure the company's continued legal compliance.

Overall, the role of corporate counsel involves navigating complex and multifaceted scenarios where legal risks must be carefully weighed against potential rewards. This balancing act requires a combination of legal expertise, business acumen, ethical judgment, and effective communication skills.

Legal Counsel's Bigger Role

Legal counsel, both in-house and outside counsel, is playing a more significant role in strategy and innovation. Businesses are increasingly relying on their legal team to help them identify opportunities to increase revenue and decrease cost and risk. There has been a considerable shift in forward-thinking companies from viewing legal counsel as a stumbling block to more of a strategic partner taking on larger and more strategic roles within organizations. Here are some ways in which legal counsel's roles have been expanding:

- **Strategic Advisers:** Corporate counsel are not just legal experts; they are becoming strategic advisers to senior management and the board of directors. They provide legal insights on business decisions, risk management, and overall corporate strategy. Their input helps ensure that legal considerations are integrated into the organization's broader goals.

- **Risk Management:** Corporate counsel play a critical role in identifying, assessing, and managing legal and regulatory risks that the company might face. They help develop risk mitigation strategies and ensure compliance with laws and regulations to avoid potential legal pitfalls.

- **Contract Management:** Corporate counsel are often responsible for drafting, reviewing, and negotiating contracts with clients, vendors, partners, and other stakeholders. Their involvement ensures that contracts are legally sound and aligned with the company's interests.

- **Litigation Management:** If legal disputes arise, in-house counsel coordinate and manage the organization's response to litigation or other legal actions. They may work closely with external law firms, oversee litigation strategies, and assess settlement options.

- **Intellectual Property Protection:** Protecting intellectual property (IP) assets, such as patents, trademarks, and copyrights, is crucial for many companies. Corporate counsel help safeguard these assets by managing IP portfolios, enforcing rights, and defending against infringement claims.

- **Mergers and Acquisitions (M&A):** Corporate counsel play a significant role in due diligence and legal aspects of M&A transactions. They assess legal risks associated with potential acquisitions, negotiate terms, and ensure a smooth transition post-acquisition.

- **Data Privacy and Cybersecurity:** With the increasing importance of data privacy and cybersecurity, corporate counsel are involved in crafting policies, procedures, and compliance measures to protect sensitive information and ensure compliance with data protection laws.

- **Ethics and Corporate Governance:** Corporate counsel help uphold ethical standards and ensure adherence to corporate governance practices. They assist in drafting codes of conduct, handling whistleblower complaints, and promoting transparency within the organization.

- **Internal Investigations:** In case of allegations of misconduct or policy violations within the company, corporate counsel may lead internal investigations to assess the situation, gather evidence, and determine appropriate actions.

- **Employee Training:** Corporate counsel often contribute to employee training programs related to legal and compliance matters. This helps ensure that all employees are aware of the legal implications of their actions and responsibilities.

Here are some additional tips for lawyers who balance legal risks with company business strategies:

- **Be a trusted advisor.** Lawyers should build relationships with business leaders and become trusted advisors. This will help lawyers to be more effective in communicating legal risks and developing risk mitigation strategies.

- **Be flexible.** The legal landscape is constantly changing, so lawyers need to be flexible in their approach to risk management. They need to be able to adapt their strategies to changing circumstances.

- **Be creative.** There is often more than one way to mitigate a legal risk. Lawyers should be creative in their thinking and come up with solutions that are tailored to the specific needs of the company without hindering business growth.

- **Be collaborative.** Lawyers should work with other professionals, such as accountants, insurance brokers, and risk managers, to develop comprehensive risk management plans.

The role of corporate counsel can vary based on the industry, company size, and specific legal challenges faced by the organization. Successful companies have their internal business operations partner with legal counsel to ensure lawyers get early signals of potential legal risk. There is no doubt that it is critical for legal counsel to have a seat at the table to be able to balance legal risks with business strategies.

Product Counsel:

Another example of how legal counsel is partnering with the organization's stakeholders is through the role of product counsel. The most effective product counsel have a deep understanding of product goals early, which helps them to identify and address legal issues more quickly and accurately. By working closely with the product team through development, updates, and deployment, they can not only provide legal guidance, but help advance projects as they address potential risks.

Building Boldness through Preparedness

Building a bold business strategy through legal risk preparedness requires a well-thought-out approach that balances innovation with legal caution, ensuring the long-term success and sustainability of any organization. Integrating legal risk management into business strategy can mitigate potential challenges and create a more resilient and forward-thinking organization. This approach ensures the business is equipped to adapt, pivot, and thrive in a rapidly changing environment. Steps to consider:

Thorough Research and Analysis:

- Gather comprehensive data about the industry, market trends, competitors, and customer preferences.

- Conduct a SWOT analysis (Strengths, Weaknesses, Opportunities, Threats) to identify potential areas of growth and vulnerability.

Understand Goals:

- Understand business objectives and goals. What does the organization aim to achieve with bold moves?

Risk Assessment and Mitigation:

- Identify potential legal risks associated with bold strategies.

- Prioritize these risks based on their potential impact and likelihood. (Discussed in *Chapter 3—Legal Risk Management*)

- Develop contingency plans to address the identified risks. What steps can be taken if things don't go as planned?

Pilot Programs:

- Before fully implementing a bold strategy, consider running pilot programs to assess their feasibility and potential outcomes.

- Use the results to gather real-world data and make informed adjustments.

Flexibility and Adaptability:

- Be prepared to adjust the legal risk mitigation strategy if new information emerges or if the situation changes.

- Maintain the ability to pivot if the bold move is yielding higher than expected legal risks.

Bold but Not Reckless

Understand that being bold doesn't mean being reckless. By carefully considering the legal risks, conducting thorough research, and implementing strategic safeguards, innovative and daring business strategies can be pursued while maintaining a prudent approach.

Examples of Balancing Legal Risks with Business Strategies

- **Product Development and Liability:** A technology company developing a new software application must consider potential legal risks, such as intellectual property infringement or privacy violations. To balance these risks with their business strategy, the company should have legal counsel review and assess patents and privacy policies, ensuring that their product complies with relevant laws and regulations.

- **Contract Negotiations:** A manufacturing company entering into a contract with a supplier in a foreign country must navigate legal risks related to international trade, intellectual property protection, and dispute resolution. To balance these risks with their business strategy, the company can work with legal experts who are knowledgeable in the laws of the target country to draft a contract that is applicable to the laws of the country and outlines clear terms and dispute resolution mechanisms for enforceability.

- **Data Privacy and Cybersecurity:** An e-commerce company collecting customer data for marketing purposes needs to balance their business strategy with legal risks related to data privacy. To achieve this balance, they can invest in robust cybersecurity measures, implement clear privacy policies, and comply with data protection regulations, including the General Data Protection Regulation (GDPR), California Consumer Privacy Act (CCPA), or similar regulations.

- **Expansion into New Markets:** When expanding into new markets, companies encounter varying legal and regulatory landscapes. To balance legal risks with business strategies, a company can conduct thorough market research, consult with legal experts who understand applicable regulations, and adapt their business model to align with the legal requirements of the new markets.

- **Mergers and Acquisitions:** When considering mergers or acquisitions, companies must assess legal risks associated with financial liabilities, regulatory compliance, and potential lawsuits. They can balance these risks with business strategies by conducting thorough due diligence, involving legal counsel, and structuring the deal to align with business objectives while mitigating identified risks.

- **Advertising and Marketing:** A company planning an advertising campaign must navigate legal risks related to false advertising, trademark infringement, and consumer protection laws. To strike a balance, legal counsel should review marketing materials before the campaign launch to ensure compliance with advertising regulations.

- **Environmental Compliance:** A manufacturing company striving to minimize its environmental impact while maximizing profits needs to balance environmental regulations with their business strategy. They can achieve this balance by investing in sustainable practices, obtaining necessary permits, and monitoring their operations' compliance with environmental laws.

- **Intellectual Property Protection:** An agency creating original content must consider legal risks related to copyright and trademark infringement. Balancing these risks with business strategies involves registering trademarks and copyrights, ensuring proper licensing agreements, researching potential risks of infringement on another's intellectual property, and actively monitoring for unauthorized use of their own.

- **Supply Chain Management:** Companies relying on complex supply chains should be aware of legal risks related to labor practices, human rights violations, and environmental impact in their supply chain. Balancing these risks with business strategies involves conducting due diligence on suppliers, implementing codes of conduct, and working to address any identified issues that could impede business growth.

In all the above scenarios, the key is to integrate legal considerations into business strategies from the outset rather than treating legal risk mitigation as an afterthought. Collaboration between legal experts and business leaders is essential for achieving a balanced approach that minimizes legal risks while facilitating the company's growth and success.

Case Study Examples of Balancing Legal Risks with Business Strategies

Many major companies have had to balance legal risks with their business strategies in order to navigate complex regulatory environments, potential lawsuits, and other legal challenges. Some examples include:

Amazon:

Amazon navigates a complex web of legal challenges while pursuing its aggressive business expansion. Here are some notable examples showcasing how Amazon balances legal risks with its business strategies:

1. Antitrust Concerns and Market Dominance:

- **Legal Risk: Potential liability associated with** allegations of stifling competition through exclusive deals with suppliers, predatory pricing, and self-preferencing on its marketplace.

- **Business Strategy:** Amazon mitigated antitrust allegations by making minor adjustments to its business practices, such as offering Prime membership benefits to competing sellers. Amazon has also intensified its lobbying efforts, engaging with policymakers to shape regulatory discussion related to antitrust. Further, Amazon has diversified its business portfolio beyond e-commerce into areas like cloud computing, entertainment (Amazon Prime Video), smart devices (Amazon Echo), and logistics, aiming to demonstrate that the company operates in competitive markets and faces rivals in multiple sectors.

2. Labor Practices and Worker Rights:

- **Legal Risk:** Liability for harsh working conditions in warehouse facilities, leading to lawsuits and unionization efforts.

- **Business Strategy:** Amazon invested in automation and robotics to streamline operations and reduce dependency on human labor to minimize labor-related liability. Amazon increased its minimum wage and introduced employee benefits, including health insurance, career training initiatives, and tuition reimbursement. Amazon is continuously working to improve its workplace environment by implementing feedback mechanisms, conducting safety training, and making changes to its policies based on internal and external reviews. Balancing legal risks with its business strategy has not affected Amazon's expansive growth.

3. Counterfeit Products and Brand Protection:

- **Legal Risk:** Balancing the convenience of its online marketplace with preventing liability for the sale of counterfeit knockoff products.

- **Business Strategy:** Amazon implemented automated scanning algorithms to detect counterfeit listings, cooperating with brands to remove infringing products, and holding sellers accountable through suspensions and financial penalties.

4. Tax Optimization and Global Revenue Sharing:

- **Legal Risk:** Liability related to aggressive tax avoidance strategies and shifting profits to low-tax jurisdictions.

- **Business Strategy:** Amazon adjusted its corporate structure while cooperating with tax authorities and policymakers in various countries to shape related regulatory discussion.

5. Data Privacy and Consumer Protection:

- **Legal Risk:** Liability for the collection and analysis of user data with privacy concerns and regulations including the General Data Protection Regulation (GDPR) enforced in the EU.

- **Business Strategy:** Implementing transparency tools for users to control data collection and usage, offering opt-out options for targeted advertising, and working with regulators to comply with data privacy laws. Amazon continues to strike a successful balance between the legal risk of customer data privacy protections and its desire to leverage customer data for business growth.

These examples highlight the delicate balancing act Amazon performs between maximizing growth and managing legal risks. While the company has implemented various strategies to mitigate these risks, here are some key approaches:

- **Active Lobbying and Engagement:** Amazon proactively influences regulations and collaborates with authorities to shape rules in its favor.

- **Investments in Compliance and Technology:** The company dedicates resources to legal compliance and leverages technology to automate compliance monitoring.

- **Minor Adjustments and Adaptability:** While defending its core business model, Amazon makes strategic adjustments to comply with regulations and appease authorities.

- **Focus on Growth and Market Dominance:** Despite legal hurdles, Amazon prioritizes expansion and market leadership, often pushing boundaries and facing anticipated consequences later.

Amazon has demonstrated a combination of reactive and proactive strategies when balancing on the tightrope between legal risk and business strategy while maintaining its growth momentum.

Apple:

Apple navigates a complex business landscape, and its success hinges on its ability to balance potential legal risks with its business strategy. Here are a few notable examples:

1. App Store Antitrust:

- **Legal Risk:** Apple faced antitrust scrutiny for allegedly using its App Store as a monopoly, forcing developers to use its payment system, controlling app distribution, and restricting competition.

- **Business Strategy:** While maintaining App Store control, Apple made concessions to appease regulators and developers. Apple lowered commission fees for smaller developers, allowed external links within certain apps, and introduced App Store Search Ads for fairer competition. Additionally, Apple allowed developers to inform users about alternative payment options outside the app.

2. Data Privacy Concerns:

- **Legal Risk:** Regulatory scrutiny and investigations regarding data collection and user privacy, particularly with features like iMessage and iCloud.

- **Business Strategy:** Apple revised policies to emphasize strong data security and user control, enhanced disclosures to detail privacy explanations, empowered users to manage their data, and used advanced encryption technologies to protect user data. Additionally, Apple collaborated with governments on data security initiatives to help shape regulations in line with its business objectives.

3. Intellectual Property Disputes:

- **Legal Risk:** Numerous patent lawsuits with competitors like Samsung and Huawei, potentially hindering product development and sales.

- **Business Strategy:** Apple aggressively protected its intellectual property through patents and copyrights. To balance legal risks with its business strategies, Apple engaged in cross-licensing agreements with various companies to reduce legal battles and ensure technology access.

4. Environmental and Labor Practices:

- **Legal Risk:** Liability concerns related to working conditions in Apple's supply chain and the environmental impact of its manufacturing processes.

- **Business Strategy:** Apple implemented stricter supplier code of conduct guidelines and conducted regular audits to ensure compliance, as well as invested in clean energy initiatives. Apple also published detailed supplier responsibility reports to demonstrate transparency and invested in product longevity and ease of recycling as a conciliatory gesture.

5. Right to Repair Controversy:

- **Legal Risk:** Proposed legislation demanding that Apple provide repair parts and manuals to consumers, potentially impacting profits and control over product maintenance.

- **Business Strategy:** Apple argued for security and quality concerns of independent repairs, but mitigated the controversy by offering certified repair programs and partnered with some service providers.

These examples illustrate how Apple balances legal risks with its business strategies by employing a multi-pronged approach:

- **Proactive Compliance:** Implementing policies and practices that meet both legal and ethical standards as well as promote its business objectives.

- **Transparency and Communication:** Openly communicating its actions in public relations announcements and addressing concerns of stakeholders.

- **Strategic Concessions:** Adapting its business practices where necessary to mitigate legal risks while minimizing impact on core principles and ongoing innovation.

- **Investment in Innovation:** Developing new technologies and processes that enhance user experience and security, potentially reducing legal vulnerabilities.

Balancing legal risks with business strategies is an ongoing challenge for Apple, but its adaptability and proactive approach have proven crucial in maintaining its success in a dynamic and complex business environment.

Alphabet Inc. (Google):

Google has faced various legal challenges over the years related to its dominant position in online search and advertising. Google walks a tightrope between pushing business boundaries and complying with a complex web of legal regulations. The company balances legal risks with its business strategies in order to manage regulatory compliance, antitrust allegations, and potential fines. While navigating these risks isn't always smooth sailing, Google's calculated ventures have often yielded significant business success. Here are some notable examples showcasing how Google masterfully balances legal risks with its business strategies:

1. Data Privacy and Targeted Advertising:

- **Legal Risk:** Allegations of privacy law violations related to personalized advertising, a core revenue stream for Google.

- **Business Strategy:** Implementing robust data security measures, offering granular user control over data collection and ad personalization. Key is actively engaging with regulators to shape privacy standards. Google's innovative privacy sandbox initiative explores alternative ad targeting methods that minimize reliance on personal data.

2. Copyright Battles and Content Protection:

- **Legal Risk:** Infringement of protected copyrighted content and enabling user access to information.

- **Business Strategy:** Google's subsidiary, YouTube, implemented the Content ID system to identify and monetize copyrighted content uploaded to YouTube, sharing revenue with creators while keeping users engaged. Balancing copyright protection with the freedom of expression for users has been an ongoing challenge.

3. Antitrust Scrutiny and Market Dominance:

- **Legal Risk:** Facing antitrust investigations in various countries over alleged monopolistic practices in search and advertising.

- **Business Strategy:** Google adjusted its products and services, including search algorithms, advertising policies, and user data handling to address legal concerns. Google also altered its search results in the EU to include more prominent links to rival shopping comparison services.

4. Ethical Considerations and AI Development:

- **Legal Risk:** Legal concerns related to bias and discrimination in AI algorithms used in products like facial recognition and search ranking.

- **Business Strategy:** Implementing fairness audits and establishing ethical guidelines for AI development.

Google's AI principles and practices emphasize responsible development and deployment of AI technology.

5. Geopolitical Tensions and Data Localization:

- **Legal Risk:** Navigating data localization laws in various countries, which can hinder the free flow of information and innovation.

- **Business Strategy:** Advocating for open data flows and working with local governments to find compliant solutions. Google also invested in building local data centers in some regions to specifically comply with local laws.

These are just a few examples of how Google navigates the intricate legal landscape while pursuing its ambitious business goals. The company's success in balancing legal risks with its business strategies can be attributed to its:

- **Proactive Approach:** Google often anticipates legal challenges and takes steps to mitigate risks before they materialize.

- **Transparency and Engagement:** Google actively engages with regulators, stakeholders, and the public to address concerns and build trust as well as works to shape regulations to align with its business objectives.

- **Investment in Compliance:** Google dedicates significant resources to legal compliance and ethical practices.

Google has engaged in significant public relations campaigns to portray itself as an innovator benefiting consumers and the economy. This proactive lobbying campaign is intended to potentially influence policymakers and possibly shape antitrust regulations to balance such legal risks with Google's business strategies.

Meta Platforms, Inc. (Facebook):

Meta, formerly known as Facebook, has encountered numerous legal challenges involving user privacy, data breaches, and antitrust investigations. Balancing these legal risks with its business strategies has been a complex and ongoing process for the company. Here are some examples of how Meta has attempted to achieve this equilibrium:

1. Targeted Advertising and Data Privacy:

- **Legal Risk:** Meta's core business model relies heavily on targeted advertising, which utilizes user data for personalization. This practice creates legal risks relating to privacy law violations and has sparked legal battles surrounding data collection and usage.

- **Business Strategy:** Meta implemented several measures to balance these legal risks with their business strategies, including introducing more granular privacy controls that allow users to control different types of access to information according to their identity, role, attributes, or level of security clearance. Additionally, Meta has offered data download options and established independent oversight boards. Meta also invested in anonymization technologies and differential privacy research to minimize the risk of individual re-identification from aggregated data. With minimal impact to its operations, Meta adjusted its business practices to align with data privacy laws around the world, such as the General Data Protection Regulation (GDPR) in Europe and the California

Consumer Privacy Act (CCPA) in the United States, thus balancing these legal risks with its business strategies.

2. Content Moderation and Freedom of Speech:

- **Legal Risk:** Meta's platforms host a vast amount of user-generated content, raising the complex issue of balancing freedom of expression with content moderation responsibilities. The company has faced legal challenges for both removing content and failing to remove content deemed harmful or offensive by some.

- **Business Strategy:** Meta established content moderation policies and guidelines that attempt to strike a balance between protecting users from harmful content and upholding freedom of expression. The company employs a combination of automated tools and human reviewers to identify and remove violating content to mitigate the risk of legal liability for illegal or harmful content posted by users. Additionally, Meta implemented transparency measures such as content removal reports and appeals processes as part of its plan to demonstrate that it is not restricting speech, thus balancing legal risks with its business strategies to support Meta's expansive growth.

3. Competition and Antitrust Concerns:

- **Legal Risk:** Meta's dominant position in the social media market has drawn scrutiny from antitrust regulators, who allege that the company may be abusing its market power to stifle competition.

- **Business Strategy:** Meta addressed these concerns by divesting certain assets, such as Giphy, and working with antitrust investigations. Additionally, the company advocated for industry-wide regulations that would create a more level playing field for all social media companies.

These examples demonstrate the ongoing challenges faced by Meta in balancing its business strategy with legal and ethical considerations. The company has dealt with legal risks that directly intersect with its business strategies by adapting policies, practices, and technologies to mitigate legal risks while continuing its operations and growth. As regulators and users alike continue to scrutinize Meta's practices, the company continues to evolve and find innovative ways to uphold and pursue its core business objectives while minimizing legal risks.

<u>Microsoft</u>:

Microsoft has encountered various legal challenges relating to antitrust issues, patent disputes, and privacy concerns. The company has adapted its business strategy to manage compliance with legal requirements and maintain positive relationships with regulators. Here are some key examples showcasing how Microsoft has balanced legal risks with its business strategies:

1. Open-Source Antitrust Allegations:

- **Legal Risk:** In the 1990s and early 2000s, Microsoft faced antitrust scrutiny for allegedly stifling open-source software (OSS) competition. Microsoft faced several legal challenges related to its dominance in the operating systems market.

- **Business Strategy:** Microsoft adopted a more open approach, contributing to and collaborating with OSS projects. This mitigated legal risks and fostered developer goodwill, leading to Microsoft becoming a major contributor to OSS projects. Microsoft also made changes in how it packaged and released its Windows operating system. For instance, Microsoft offered versions of Windows without its own browser, allowing users to choose their preferred web browser. The company then shifted focus toward cloud computing to reduce reliance on its Windows operating system. Microsoft's diversification of its products highlights the balancing act of navigating legal challenges while continuing with innovative business strategies to deal with its market dominance.

2. Data Privacy Liabilities:

- **Legal Risk:** Allegations of privacy law and data security violations related to cloud computing.

- **Business Strategy:** Microsoft implemented robust data privacy measures, including transparency tools and user control options. It also actively engaged with policymakers to help shape privacy regulations. Microsoft's cloud platform is now recognized for its strong privacy and security practices, attracting customers concerned about data protection.

3. Antitrust Battles:

- **Legal Risk:** Microsoft has a long history of antitrust investigations and lawsuits related to its dominant market position.

- **Business Strategy:** Microsoft adopted a more conciliatory approach, working with regulators to address competition concerns. It also diversified its product offerings to reduce reliance on Windows. Balancing antitrust legal risks with its business strategies has allowed Microsoft to avoid major sanctions and continue to operate successfully.

4. Ethical AI Development:

- **Legal Risk:** Artificial intelligence (AI) raised liability and ethical concerns around bias, transparency, and accountability.

- **Business Strategy:** Microsoft established principles for responsible AI development, focusing on fairness, transparency, and accountability. It also launched initiatives to mitigate bias and promote explainable AI.

5. Cybersecurity Liabilities:

- **Legal Risk:** Cyberattacks posed a significant threat to Microsoft's business and reputation. Legal liabilities could arise from data breaches or security failures.

- **Business Strategy:** Microsoft invested heavily in cybersecurity research and development, offering robust security solutions for businesses and individuals. Microsoft also collaborated with governments to help shape regulations to combat cybercrime while considering its business strategy. In certain countries, Microsoft established regional data centers to comply with local laws regarding data storage and privacy rather than attempt to challenge the regional regulatory inconsistencies.

6. Patent Liabilities:

- **Legal Risk:** Microsoft has been involved in numerous patent litigation cases as both plaintiff and defendant.

- **Business Strategy:** To mitigate legal risks, Microsoft strategically used its patent portfolio to enter cross-licensing agreements with other companies. These arrangements not only helped to mitigate legal liability, but also generated revenue from licensing its intellectual property.

These examples demonstrate Microsoft's ongoing efforts to balance legal risks with its business strategies. By balancing compliance, ethical practices, and user trust with its business objectives, Microsoft navigates this complex legal landscape while pursuing its ambitious goals.

Tesla:

Tesla has a history of taking bold legal risks in pursuit of its business goals. Tesla has encountered legal challenges related to securities regulations, autopilot technology, and manufacturing practices. The company's business strategy has been influenced by legal risks in the fast-evolving automotive and technology sectors. Here are some noteworthy examples showcasing how Tesla has balanced legal risks with its business strategies:

1. Autopilot and Full Self-Driving (FSD):

- **Legal Risk:** Liability resulting from accidents involving Tesla vehicles equipped with Autopilot or FSD, as well as regulatory scrutiny from the National Highway Traffic Safety Administration (NHTSA) and the National Transportation Safety Board (NTSB).

- **Business Strategy:** Tesla took steps to improve Autopilot and FSD technology safety, while also strategically shifting potential liability to the driver by conducting training emphasizing that the driver must remain attentive while using the Autopilot and FSD feature.

2. Gigafactories and Environmental Impact:

- **Legal Risk:** Tesla's rapid expansion through Gigafactories has drawn attention to its environmental impact, including water usage and battery recycling. The company has faced regulatory hurdles and legal liability.

- **Business Strategy:** Tesla partnered with local communities to address environmental concerns relating to its Gigafactories as they invested in renewable energy sources and battery recycling technologies. Tesla's goal for balancing legal risks with its business strategies is to assure its sustainability by aligning its brand image with environmentally responsible initiatives that attract environmentally conscious customers.

3. Labor Practices and Worker Rights:

- **Legal Risk:** Tesla has faced criticism for its labor practices, including allegations of union-busting and worker injuries. The company has been sued by the National Labor Relations Board (NLRB) and faces threats of regulatory intervention.

- **Business Strategy:** Tesla has taken steps to improve its labor practices, including offering higher wages and benefits without third-party involvement. Tesla emphasizes safety training and has established a grievance process for workers to be heard. Balancing worker rights (legal risks) with production goals (business strategy) remains an objective for the company.

4. Data Privacy and Security:

- **Legal Risk:** Tesla collects a vast amount of data from its vehicles and customers, raising concerns about data privacy and security. The company has faced data breaches and regulatory scrutiny in Europe and other regions.

- **Business Strategy:** Tesla provided customers with control over their data and outlined its data collection practices in its privacy policy for transparency. Tesla continues to balance data security legal risks with its business strategies to build trust with customers and keep regulators at bay in this area.

5. Vehicle Quality and Consumer Protection Lawsuits:

- **Legal Risk:** Tesla encountered legal challenges relating to vehicle defects and malfunctioning systems.

- **Business Strategy:** Tesla addressed these concerns by adding warranty services, recall initiatives, and improving quality control. Tesla has balanced legal risks with its business strategies by demonstrating the company's commitment to resolving issues promptly and enhancing product quality.

In each example, Tesla sought to balance legal risks by implementing a strategy that aligned with its business goals and commitments whether by improving technology, complying with regulations, addressing labor concerns, enhancing product quality, or safeguarding user interests. Balancing legal risks with business strategies is an ongoing challenge for Tesla. However, its proactive approach and commitment to innovation have allowed Tesla to achieve significant success in the electric vehicle and clean energy markets.

Uber:

Uber's meteoric rise has been riddled with legal challenges relating to data privacy and its classification of drivers as independent contractors, forcing the company to constantly walk the tightrope between legal risk and its aggressive business strategy. Here are some examples showcasing how Uber has balanced legal risks with its business strategies:

1. "Greyball" - Defying Regulation:

- **Legal Risk:** Early on, Uber's "Greyball" program used sophisticated algorithms to identify and evade authorities in cities where its operations were banned. This raised concerns about illegal operations and lack of transparency.

- **Business Strategy:** Uber shifted toward a more collaborative approach, engaging with policymakers and regulators to address concerns as it continued its business expansion without interruption. Uber implemented transparency measures like trip data sharing with cities. Uber's approach to balancing legal risks with its business strategies has helped it gain legitimacy in many markets.

2. Worker Classification:

- **Legal Risk:** Uber's classification of drivers as independent contractors rather than employees sparked legal battles worldwide. This strategy created liability for misclassification of its drivers, thus denying drivers of benefits like minimum wage, overtime pay, and unemployment insurance.

- **Business Strategy:** Uber creatively defended its position, arguing that its model offers flexibility and economic opportunity for part-time, freelance drivers as part of the new "gig" economy. Uber then implemented alternative business models like employee leasing in certain markets to address concerns about driver welfare. Additionally, Uber adjusted its model in some regions, providing drivers with certain benefits or creating new worker classifications without full employee status. Uber continues to push the limits to keep the debate over worker classification unresolved as it pursues its aggressive growth plans.

3. Data Privacy:

- **Legal Risk:** Uber collects vast amounts of user data, including location history and trip details. This creates legal risks related to privacy law violations and potential misuse of data.

- **Business Strategy:** Uber has implemented data privacy measures like anonymization and user control over data sharing. It also implemented a more transparent practice relating to data collection and usage practices.

These are just a few examples of how Uber has balanced legal risks with its business strategies in the complex landscape of its business growth. The company's ability to adapt, collaborate, and innovate will be key to its continued success in a rapidly evolving regulatory environment.

Walmart:

Walmart has navigated various legal risks while maintaining a robust business strategy. Here are some examples illustrating how it has balanced legal risks with its business strategies:

1. Labor and Employment Practices:

- **Legal Risk:** Walmart faced various lawsuits regarding wage and hour violations.

- **Business Strategy:** Walmart adjusted its policies and practices, implementing changes in wage structures and overtime rules to comply with labor laws in a manner that had minimal impact on operations.

2. Product Liability and Safety:

- **Legal Risk:** Walmart faced potential liabilities related to defective products.

- **Business Strategy:** Walmart implemented stringent quality control measures, collaborated with suppliers to ensure product safety, and also shifted potential liability by maintaining liability insurance, thus balancing legal risks while upholding a commitment to its business strategy.

3. Environmental Regulations:

- **Legal Risks:** Walmart faced allegations of environmental regulatory violations.

- **Business Strategies:** Walmart implemented business sustainability initiatives that included efforts to reduce its carbon footprint and use renewable energy in certain areas. This approach not only reduced Walmart's legal risks associated with non-compliance with environmental regulations, but was also leveraged as a promotion for Walmart's commitment to environmental sustainability.

4. Data Privacy and Security:

- **Legal Risk:** There has been an increasing focus on Walmart's data privacy and security practices and allegations of noncompliance with data protection laws.

- **Business Strategy:** Walmart has taken steps to enhance cybersecurity measures, comply with data protection laws, and safeguard customer information. Walmart obtained customer consent for data collection and also provided customers with clear options for managing their privacy settings and control of how their data is used. This approach not only mitigated legal risks related to data privacy and collection, but also reinforced customer trust, and was promoted as a strategic initiative to provide a secure shopping experience.

5. Antitrust and Competition Laws:

- **Legal Risks:** Walmart has faced scrutiny over potential antitrust concerns.

- **Business Strategy:** Walmart engaged in initiatives supporting local suppliers and small businesses, showcasing a commitment to fair competition. This strategy mitigated the legal risks associated with allegations of monopolistic behavior.

These examples demonstrate how Walmart has adopted a balanced approach between legal risks and its business strategy to ensure its competitive edge and long-term success.

The concept of being bold but cautious emphasizes that while taking bold actions can lead to significant business outcomes, it's important to do so with a thoughtful and cautious approach of being aware of potential pitfalls, doing research, planning, and making informed decisions before taking action to minimize potential legal risks or negative outcomes.

Achieving the right balance between legal risks and business strategy requires collaboration between legal experts and business leaders to identify, assess, and manage legal risks while pursuing strategic goals. By prioritizing legal considerations alongside business objectives, companies can minimize potential setbacks and create a more resilient and prosperous business model.

CHAPTER 2
What Are Legal Risks?

Legal risks are the potential for financial or reputational harm to a business resulting from non-compliance with laws, regulations, contractual obligations, or engaging in negligent or intentional business misconduct. Risks are caused by internal errors, flawed processes, lack of oversight, negligence, and deliberate conduct. Legal risk can also result from a lack of complete knowledge of the laws and regulations applicable to the business.

Approaching legal risks solely from a defensive standpoint can hinder business growth and innovation. Thus, striking a balance between legal risks and strategic business objectives becomes crucial for long-term success.

Corporate counsel, whether in-house or external legal counsel, are increasingly proactive in managing legal risks to protect company and shareholder interests. But to accomplish that goal, it is necessary to have a structured way of **identifying**, **assessing**, and **mitigating** legal risks.

Identifying Legal Risks

Identifying legal risks in business is crucial for proactive risk management and ensuring compliance with applicable laws and regulations. Legal risks can vary depending on the industry and jurisdiction, but here are some common legal risks that businesses may face:

Regulatory Risk:

Businesses are subject to a wide range of complex and ever-evolving laws and regulations, both federal and state, specific to their industry. Failure to comply with these requirements can result in fines, penalties, civil actions, or even criminal charges.

Litigation Risk:

The risk of being sued is inescapable. Companies face a range of events that can cause litigation. Customers can bring a lawsuit for product liability, discrimination, personal injury for on-premises accidents, bad faith, malpractice, etc. Employees can bring legal action for wrongful termination, discrimination, wage-hour violations, harassment, work-related injuries, poor working conditions, or breach of contract. To further pile on, certain situations can result in the business being liable for the actions of their employees and third-party vendors.

Contractual Risk:

Entering into contracts without proper review or understanding of contractual complexities can lead to legal disputes, harmful liability, breach of contract claims, or financial losses.

Poorly drafted or ambiguous contracts can lead to disputes and potential legal liabilities. Many businesses use standard form contract provisions that are not favorable to them. It is critical that legal counsel ensure that contracts with customers, suppliers, employees, and partners are clear, legally binding, and address all necessary terms, including but not limited to payment terms, intellectual property rights, confidentiality, liability limitations, dispute resolution mechanisms, damages provisions, contract termination, and governing law. Moreover, businesses must pay close attention not to enter into contracts where they lack bargaining power and where contractual obligations can pose future difficulties for the business.

Intellectual Property Risk:

Businesses must not only protect their own intellectual property rights, such as trademarks, copyrights, patents, and trade secrets; conversely, they must not also infringe on the intellectual property rights of others or can be sued for damages.

Unauthorized use of trademarks, copyrights, patents, or trade secrets can lead to legal action and significant financial damages. It is important to conduct thorough searches and due diligence to ensure the company's products, services, or branding do not infringe upon the intellectual property rights of others.

Advertising and Statements Risk:

Businesses must be careful not to engage in false advertising and make false or misleading statements to customers, investors, or the public. Such statements can lead to lawsuits for fraud or misrepresentation.

Employment Practices Risk:

Businesses must comply with a variety of state and federal labor laws governing employment, such as those relating to discrimination, wage-hour violations, occupational health and safety laws, harassment, and wrongful termination. Failure to do so can lead to lawsuits and significant fines and penalties. It is important to mitigate legal risks by establishing proper policies and procedures, including fair hiring practices, employment contracts, workplace safety measures, and employee training programs.

Product Liability Risk:

If a business manufactures or sells products, there is a risk of product defects, inadequate warnings or instructions, or failure to meet safety standards. Product liability claims can result in costly litigation, recalls, and damage to the company's reputation, goodwill, and brand value.

Environmental Liability Risk:

Businesses that pollute the environment or fail to comply with environmental regulations can be held liable for cleanup costs, fines, reputational damage, and other damages.

Data Privacy and Security Risk:

With increased digitalization, businesses must protect sensitive customer data and comply with applicable data protection laws, and applicable state privacy laws. It is critical for an organization to implement robust data security measures, privacy policies, and consent mechanisms to safeguard personal information.

Data Breaches Risk:

Businesses that suffer data breaches or cyber-attacks can be sued by customers whose personal information is compromised, and the company can also be subject to regulatory penalties. Mishandling or unauthorized access to customer or employee data can also result in reputational damage and loss of customer trust.

With increased digitalization, businesses must protect sensitive customer data and comply with applicable data protection laws. It is critical to implement robust data security measures, privacy policies, and consent mechanisms to safeguard personal information.

Insider Data Security Risk:

Employees, contractors, or individuals with legitimate access to systems can intentionally or unintentionally compromise data security. Insider threats can arise from negligence, lack of training, disgruntled employees, or other motivations. It is important to implement strict access controls and least privilege principles, ensuring that only authorized individuals can access specific data and systems limited to their job responsibilities.

Antitrust and Competition Legal Risk:

Engaging in anti-competitive behavior, such as price-fixing, bid-rigging, or monopolistic practices, can lead to investigations by competition and government authorities, resulting in potential legal action, losses, and fines.

Tax and Financial Compliance Risk:

Non-compliance with tax regulations, fraudulent accounting practices, or misrepresentation of financial information can lead to audits, penalties, legal actions, and reputational harm.

Anti-Corruption Laws Risk:

Dealing with foreign officials must not involve payments, gifts, or other business courtesies for the benefit of your company. It is crucial to comply with anti-corruption laws, such as the Foreign Corrupt Practices Act (FCPA) or the UK Bribery Act, which prohibit bribery and unethical practices. The FCPA targets corruption and bribery for paying foreign officials to expedite legal processes or obtain contracts. The Securities and Exchange Commission (SEC) and the US Department of Justice (DOJ) are jointly responsible for enforcing the FCPA. Violating these laws can lead to severe legal consequences, including substantial sanctions, fines, and both civil and criminal charges. Unlike the FCPA, the UK Bribery Act covers offenses involving both public and private sectors.

To mitigate these legal risks, it's important for legal counsel to review and negotiate contracts, conduct due diligence on international transactions, and ensure compliance with relevant laws and regulations. Additionally, maintaining open communication, setting clear expectations, and conducting ongoing monitoring of foreign business dealings are essential to ensure adequate legal risk management.

Vendor Third-Party Risk:

When dealing with vendors in business, all the above legal risks must be taken into consideration. It is critical that the company has strict oversight of its vendor's business and activities because the company can potentially become liable for the actions of its vendors. Legal risks posed by third-party vendor relationships can vary depending on the nature of the business and the specific vendor relationship, but here are some common legal risks:

- **Contractual Risks:** One of the primary legal risks when dealing with vendors is related to contracts. It's essential to have clear and well-drafted contracts that outline the rights, obligations, and responsibilities of both parties. Failure to have a solid contract or a clear understanding of the terms and conditions can lead to disputes, breaches of contract, and financial loss.

- **Intellectual Property Infringement:** Working with vendors may involve sharing sensitive information or using intellectual property (IP) assets, such as trademarks, patents, or copyrighted materials. There is a risk that a vendor may infringe upon someone else's IP rights or misuse the company's IP assets. It is crucial to have proper agreements in place that protect the company's IP assets and address any potential infringement issues.

- **Non-Compliance with Regulations:** Vendors may provide products or services that need to comply with specific regulations or industry standards. If a vendor fails to meet these requirements, it can result in legal violations, fines, or damage to your company's reputation. Conduct due diligence to ensure that the vendor operates within legal boundaries and meets all compliance standards applicable to your industry and organization.

- **Data Privacy and Security:** In today's digital age, data privacy and security are major concerns. When you share sensitive customer or business data with vendors, you must ensure they have adequate safeguards in place to secure and protect that information. Failure to handle data securely can lead to data breaches, legal liability, and reputational damage.

- **Vendor Insolvency or Non-Performance:** There is always a risk that a vendor may become insolvent or fail to perform their obligations adequately. This can disrupt your company's business operations and result in financial losses. It's important to assess the financial stability and reliability of vendors before entering into agreements with them and include provisions in contracts to mitigate these risks.

These are just a few of the many legal risks that businesses face. By understanding these risks and taking steps to mitigate them, businesses can help to protect themselves from financial and reputational harm. It's important for businesses to work with their in-house legal counsel or consult with external legal counsel to implement proactive measures to mitigate and balance these legal risks with business strategies.

Inefficiency Can Contribute to Legal Risks

The cloud of inefficiency hangs over many companies. Is the company holding too many meetings or running them in an inefficient way? Are too many people weighing in on the decision? Is a committee of 10 people necessary to review the matter at hand, or are 3 enough? And what about long PowerPoint presentations and reports with hyperdetailed minutia, or can the issue just be simply explained? "Is the report adequately useful to advance corporate strategy and objectives, or does it just showcase advanced PowerPoint skills?" (Reference from *Chasing Corporate Compliance*). Business inefficiency can indeed lead to various risks and negative outcomes.

- **Streamlining Operations:** Streamlining and strengthening operational, legal, and compliance processes can improve efficiency and effectiveness so that legal risks are more easily identified, managed, and mitigated. Clarifying job functions and responsibilities and job-specific training can optimize efficiency and effectiveness.

- **Standardization:** Many organizations lack standardization. In the absence of clear, repeatable, and documented processes, businesses increase the potential for legal risk and negative outcomes.

- **Missed Opportunities:** Legal risk may be self-inflicted, brought about by an organization's own strategy and decision-making. Inefficient business operations can make a business less competitive in the marketplace, as well as less compliant with applicable laws and regulations, resulting in increased costs, waste of resources, and missed opportunities for revenue generation. Most concerning are potential fines and litigation caused by a lack of oversight. However, bad decisions should not be confused with sound decisions that simply didn't work as anticipated.

- **Employee Morale and Legal Risk:** Inefficient business practices can negatively affect employee morale and productivity. This can translate into a lack of proper oversight of the areas that can lead to legal actions and compliance violations, which can further impact overall employee morale and performance.

  To mitigate legal risks, businesses should focus on continuous improvement, adopting lean methodologies, and leveraging technology to streamline processes, automate repetitive tasks, and enhance efficiency. Regular monitoring of key risk indicators (KRIs), fostering a culture of innovation and collaboration, and investing in employee training and development are also essential steps in addressing inefficiencies and mitigating associated legal risks.

Inefficiency can impact a company's compliance with regulations and legal requirements. Failure to have robust procedures in place to adhere to industry standards, data privacy regulations, or workplace safety guidelines can result in legal penalties, lawsuits, or reputational damage. There are plenty of obstacles on the path to success. Look inward to determine whether business strategy and everyday operations are boosting business or if inefficiency is contributing to legal risk.

Assessing Legal Risks

Assessing legal risks in business is a crucial aspect of any organization's risk management strategy to proactively mitigate legal risks that could impact the company's operations, reputation, and financial health. The following is a general process for assessing legal risks in business:

Assess Potential Legal Risks:

After identifying potential legal risks applicable to your organization, industry, and location, it is important to conduct a thorough analysis of your organization's activities, operations, and industry best practices to identify deficiencies within your organization. This may include compliance with laws and regulations, contracts, intellectual property rights, employment law, data privacy concerns, environmental regulations, product liability, and any other legal aspects relevant to your organization.

In-House Legal Counsel:

The legal department must drive the risk assessment process. Legal counsel is essential in identifying and assessing legal risks and identifying specific legal risks that might not be apparent to non-legal professionals.

External Legal Counsel:

Engage with experienced external legal counsel knowledgeable in your industry to conduct a comprehensive legal risk assessment. Many times, external legal counsel can provide industry-related insights and identify potential risks that may not be apparent to internal stakeholders.

Review Regulatory Environment:

Stay updated with the regulatory environment that governs your industry and business activities. This includes federal, state, and local laws and regulations. Understanding the legal landscape will help identify compliance requirements and potential risks.

Review Business Contracts:

Thoroughly review all contracts the business is a party to, such as client agreements, vendor contracts, partnership agreements, and employment contracts. Identify potential liabilities, indemnification clauses, and areas where the business may be exposed to legal risks. It is also important to review contracts after laws and regulations change, or applicable case law develops to ensure contract provisions remain strong.

Intellectual Property Assessment:

Evaluate the company's intellectual property (IP) portfolio, including trademarks, patents, copyrights, and trade secrets. Ensure that the company's IP is adequately protected and also not infringing on the rights of others.

Data Privacy and Security:

Assess the company's data privacy and security practices to mitigate the risk of data breaches and potential legal liabilities related to data protection.

Employment Practices:

Review the company's employment practices, including hiring, termination, promotion, and workplace policies, to ensure compliance with employment laws and prevent potential lawsuits.

Environmental Compliance:

If the company's business involves handling hazardous materials or impacts the environment in any way, assess its compliance with environmental regulations to avoid potential legal issues.

Litigation History:

Analyze the company's past litigation history, if applicable. Identify recurring legal issues and take corrective actions to prevent future occurrences.

Risk Prioritization:

Not all legal risks are of the same magnitude or likelihood of occurrence. Prioritize the identified risks based on their potential impact on the organization and the likelihood of their occurrence. This will help allocate resources effectively in managing these risks.

Legal risk assessment is an ongoing process that requires constant vigilance and adaptation to the changing legal landscape and business environment. By implementing a comprehensive policy, an organization can better protect itself from legal pitfalls and enhance its overall risk management practices.

Legal Risk Assessment Frequency:

A legal risk assessment should be a regular systemic component of legal oversight and not conducted only when there is a crisis. By not conducting a legal risk assessment that identifies the areas of risk and ranks them according to level of threat, time will be wasted focusing on less critical activities. Risk ranking is critical so that higher risks are mitigated first and most aggressively!

An enterprise legal risk assessment should be conducted at least every year to ensure a consistent approach to legal oversight while, at the same time, best practices demand ongoing monitoring and analysis to validate that legal obligations and new regulatory developments are properly implemented.

An annual legal risk assessment, which should also include an assessment of third-party service providers, is a preventative measure to avoid corporate liability since the company can proactively address and promptly mitigate potential legal liabilities.

Mitigating Legal Risks

Mitigating legal risks is an essential aspect of safeguarding any business or organization. Here are some steps that may be taken to reduce potential legal liabilities:

Risk Mitigation Strategies:

Develop mitigation strategies for each identified legal risk. These strategies can include policies, procedures, and guidelines that promote compliance with relevant laws and regulations, employee training, monitoring, reporting mechanisms, and contractual protections.

Compliance Policies:

Establish robust compliance policies and procedures that outline the legal requirements relevant to your organization. These should cover areas that address applicable laws and regulations, financial reporting, data privacy, employment laws, health and safety regulations, environmental standards, etc.

Employee Training and Awareness:

Train employees on legal and compliance matters relevant to their roles. Ensure that employees, especially those in key positions, understand their responsibilities and the potential legal consequences of their actions. This will increase their awareness of potential risks and help them take appropriate actions to avoid legal pitfalls.

Monitoring and Reporting:

Implement a system to monitor ongoing legal risks and compliance with established policies. Encourage employees to report any potential legal issues they come across. Create a reporting mechanism that allows employees to raise concerns anonymously if needed. Legal risks and regulations change over time, so it's essential to continuously monitor ongoing legal risks. Stay proactive in adapting your company's business practices to remain compliant with evolving legal requirements.

Regular Legal Review:

Periodically review and update the legal risk assessment policy to adapt to changing legal landscapes, business practices, and industry norms.

Integration with Business Strategy:

Align the legal risk assessment policy with the overall business strategy. This will ensure that legal risks are considered in decision-making processes and that the organization's risk management efforts are integrated across all levels.

Employment Practices:

Implement fair employment practices and maintain compliance with labor laws. This includes ensuring fair hiring, providing a safe work environment, adhering to wage and hour regulations, and avoiding discrimination and harassment.

Contracts and Agreements:

Review and negotiate contracts carefully to protect your organization's interests and avoid potential legal disputes.

Intellectual Property Protection:

Safeguard company intellectual property through patents, trademarks, copyrights, and trade secrets. Regularly monitor and enforce IP rights to prevent infringement.

Data Privacy and Security:

If your organization collects and stores customer data, ensure that you have robust data privacy and security measures in place. Comply with relevant data protection laws and regulations to protect sensitive information.

Insurance Coverage:

Assess insurance needs and invest in appropriate coverage to mitigate financial risks associated with potential legal claims.

Proper Documentation:

Maintain accurate and thorough records of all business activities, transactions, and communications. Such documentation can serve as valuable evidence in case of any legal disputes.

Dispute Resolution Strategies:

Have a clear strategy for resolving disputes with customers, suppliers, or other parties. Consider alternative dispute resolution methods like mediation or arbitration to avoid costly and time-consuming lawsuits.

Supplier and Vendor Due Diligence:

Conduct due diligence on suppliers and vendors to ensure they meet legal and compliance standards. Choose reliable partners to reduce the risk of legal complications arising from their actions.

Stay Compliant:

Ensure that your organization is compliant with all relevant laws and regulations. This may require regular audits, updating policies and procedures, and staying informed about changes in the legal landscape.

Crisis Management Plan:

Develop a crisis management plan that outlines how your organization will respond to legal challenges and crises if they materialize. This should include communication strategies and steps to contain and address the issues.

Internal Audit:

The Internal Audit Team should conduct compliance audits to assess whether the company is adhering to all applicable laws and regulations. This includes ensuring compliance with applicable state and federal regulations, employment laws, safety regulations, tax requirements, data protection laws, etc.

Board and Management Oversight:

Ensure that the board of directors and senior management are actively involved in the legal risk assessment process. They should review and approve all related policies and be updated regularly on the organization's legal risk exposure and mitigation efforts. Laws and regulations may vary depending on your company's location and industry.

Taking the above steps may help your organization minimize legal risks and operate more confidently in a complex legal environment.

CHAPTER 3
Legal Risk Management

Managing legal risks while pursuing strategic business goals is crucial for the long-term success and sustainability of any organization. Law is seldom clear-cut. Legal decisions many times involve questions such as, "Our trademark is similar to several others. But is it too similar?" Or, "Our advertising claims are not prohibited by law but still might expose us to liability. Should we proceed?" Balancing legal risks with business strategies requires not only an approach to evaluating legal risks, but also an understanding of business objectives to manage and mitigate risk with viable strategic alternatives.

Legal risk management is an important process for any business, as ongoing changes in the regulatory environment and risk landscape are constant. Mismanaging legal risk can have a significant impact on a company's financial performance, reputation, and ability to operate.

Implementing a Legal Risk Management Framework

Implementing a legal risk management framework can help evaluate, manage, and mitigate the legal risks that an organization faces.

Here are some key considerations to effectively manage legal risks:

- **Comprehensive List of Legal Risks:** The first step is to identify the legal risk categories applicable to your organization, as discussed in **Chapter 2**, and all other laws that may apply to your business and specific industry. It is essential to identify and understand the laws and regulations that apply to your organization's industry and operations, as well as the potential consequences of violating those laws. The goal is to create a comprehensive list of applicable legal risks that may impact the organization.

- **Assessing Legal Risks—Impact and Likelihood:** Once legal risks are identified, they need to be assessed in terms of their potential **impact** and **likelihood** of occurrence.

  Impact refers to the magnitude of the consequences if a risk event were to happen, while likelihood represents the probability of the risk occurring. The two key concepts of impact and likelihood help in evaluating and prioritizing risks so that higher threats of risk are mitigated first and most aggressively.

- **Impact:** Legal risks are evaluated based on their potential impact on the organization. Impact can be related to financial, operational, reputational, or other critical aspects. Impact is often expressed in qualitative or quantitative terms, and it can vary significantly from one risk to another. Here is an example of how impact can be described qualitatively:

  - Low Impact: The risk event may lead to minor consequences or insignificant disruption.

  - Moderate Impact: The risk event could cause noticeable but manageable disruptions or harm.

  - High Impact: The risk event has the potential to cause significant damage, severe consequences, or major disruption.

Assessing the potential impact of a legal risk is crucial in risk management, as it helps decision-makers understand the potential magnitude of consequences and prioritize the mitigation response accordingly.

- **Likelihood:** Likelihood, also known as probability or frequency, measures the chance or probability as a percentage of a specific risk event occurring within a given timeframe. It helps assess how likely it is for a risk to materialize. Like impact, likelihood can be expressed qualitatively or quantitatively. The qualitative scale for likelihood may include terms such as:

  - Low Likelihood: The risk event is improbable or unlikely to occur.

  - Moderate Likelihood: The risk event has a reasonable chance of occurring.

  - High Likelihood: The risk event is probable or highly likely to occur.

Risk Ranking

Risk ranking is a crucial step in legal risk management that involves assessing and prioritizing legal risks based on their potential impact and likelihood. Risk ranking is critical so that higher threats of risk are mitigated first and most aggressively. Risk ranking will also help your organization allocate resources effectively when focusing attention on the most critical risks.

Risk Ranking Methods:

There are several approaches to ranking risks based on their assessment results. Here are two commonly used methods:

- **Qualitative Risk Matrix:** A qualitative risk matrix is a visual tool that identifies and addresses risks based on their potential impact and likelihood ratings. It typically consists of impact and likelihood levels (e.g., low, medium, high) plotted on the matrix based on their assessment scores. The mitigation column determines priority. This approach provides a quick overview and helps to identify high-priority risks.

- **Quantitative Risk Scoring:** Quantitative risk scoring involves assigning numerical scores to impact and likelihood assessments. The scores can be shown individually or can be combined to calculate an overall risk score. Each risk is ranked based on its score, with higher scores indicating greater potential risk. Risks can be sorted in descending order of their scores to determine ranking.

Risk Mitigation Prioritization:

Once risks are ranked, the next step is to prioritize them. The prioritization process involves considering factors such as the severity of impact on the organization, available resources, strategic objectives, legal and regulatory requirements, and stakeholder interests. The highest-ranked risks are given the most attention and resources, while lower-ranked risks may receive less priority.

Quantitative and Qualitative Approach:

The quantitative or qualitative approach to likelihood and impact assessment is a structured methodology used to assess the probability (likelihood) of an event occurring and the potential consequences (impact) associated with that event.

The quantitative approach for impact and likelihood is the process where the person conducting the risk assessment assigns numerical probabilities to the likelihood of a risk event occurring based on their professional judgment. For instance, a 20% likelihood chance of event occurrence within a year and a 40% severity impact of the potential consequences. For example, using the quantitative approach, a risk event involving a company-wide customer data breach may be assigned a moderate likelihood number but a higher impact number than a risk event involving a failure to meet a minor contractual obligation.

By evaluating the likelihood and impact of a risk, organizations can understand how frequently they may encounter certain risks and focus on the most probable ones while also considering the severity of their potential impact.

Combining Impact and Likelihood: Risk assessment often involves combining the impact and likelihood of each identified risk to prioritize them effectively. This is usually done using a risk matrix, where the impact and likelihood are displayed in a chart. The matrix displays the risk issue categories, and ranks them on a high, medium, and low risk, based on professional judgment. For instance, a risk with high impact and high likelihood would be considered a top priority, as it poses a significant threat and is probable to occur. On the other hand, a risk with low impact and low likelihood might not require immediate attention or extensive mitigation measures.

By understanding and assessing both impact and likelihood, organizations can make informed decisions, allocate resources more efficiently, and implement appropriate risk management strategies to protect their interests and achieve their objectives. The more you know and understand about the risk the organization faces, the more effective it becomes to manage and mitigate.

Hypothetical Example of a Risk Event Involving a Legal Issue for a Software Development Company Using the Qualitative Approach

- **Task:** Evaluate and chart a potential legal risk event based on its probability of occurrence (likelihood) and potential consequences to the company (impact), using a scale of low, medium, or high to represent risk levels.

- **Potential Risk Event:** Intellectual Property Infringement Lawsuit

- **Likelihood of Occurrence:** Moderate to High

- **Impact Severity:** High

- **Priority for Mitigation:** High

Example Matrix—Likelihood and Impact

Issue	Likelihood of Occurrence	Impact Severity	Priority for Mitigation
Intellectual Property Infringement Lawsuit	Moderate to High	High	High

- **Situation:** The company is developing a new software product that incorporates some unique features. However, during the development process, they fail to conduct a thorough patent search to ensure that their innovations do not infringe upon existing patents.

- **Likelihood:** Moderate to High—The likelihood of this risk event may be considered moderate to high because the company has some basic legal procedures in place, but they lack a comprehensive review process for ensuring patent compliance.

- **Impact:** High—The impact of this risk event is high. If the company is found to have infringed upon another company's patents, it could face serious legal consequences. The impacted company may file a lawsuit seeking damages and disgorgement of any profits and may also request an injunction to stop the development and sale of the software product. This would not only result in a costly legal battle but also significant delays in the product's launch. Moreover, the company's reputation may be tarnished, leading to a loss of trust from clients and stakeholders.

Mitigation Strategy

1. **Conduct a comprehensive patent search:** The company should utilize intellectual property counsel to conduct thorough searches to identify any potential patent infringements before the software development process begins.

2. **Legal consultation:** Engage legal experts to review the software development process regularly and provide guidance on intellectual property matters.

3. **Monitor third-party contributions:** Implement strict procedures for vetting third-party code or components to ensure they do not violate any patents.

4. **Employee training:** Conduct regular training sessions for the development team to educate them about intellectual property laws and the importance of compliance.

5. **Insurance coverage:** Obtain appropriate insurance coverage to mitigate financial risks associated with legal issues if they arise.

6. **Document and communicate findings:** Present mitigation strategies in a comprehensive report that is shared with relevant stakeholders, such as senior management, board members, and other decision-makers, to ensure that they are aware of the legal risks and the recommended actions to address them.

Whether using the quantitative or qualitative approach to legal risk assessment, by proactively addressing potential harmful events and recommended mitigation strategies, the company can reduce the likelihood and potential impact of the legal risk event. Mitigation strategies may involve adjusting business practices, updating contracts, or enhancing compliance measures.

This is just a hypothetical example, and real-life scenarios are sure to have different circumstances and complexities.

The Legal Risk Matrix is a flexible and straightforward qualitative method that allows legal counsel to quickly assess, prioritize, and report on legal risks. However, it may be necessary to complement this qualitative approach for high-priority legal risks with more in-depth analysis utilizing probability percentage numbers based on professional judgment to offer a deeper understanding of potential legal consequences.

The choice of using either the qualitative or quantitative legal risk assessment depends on the context and requirements of the specific issue(s) under consideration.

Legal Risk Management Is Never "One and Done"

Remember that legal risk management is an ongoing process and never a "one-and-done" endeavor. It requires continuous vigilance and adaptation to changes in the legal landscape related to business operations. Regularly review and update the organization's legal risk management strategies, as well as revisit policies and procedures as the legal and regulatory landscape evolves and ensure that legal considerations are integrated into the decision-making processes at all levels of the organization.

Keep Pace with Changes

Legal risks and their rankings can change over time due to various factors, such as new laws and regulations, vendor relationships, new contracts, organizational changes, or external events. It is essential to regularly review and update legal risk assessments so that legal risk management strategies can be adjusted as needed to properly balance legal risks with business strategies.

Vendor Legal Risk Management

The first step in vendor legal risk management is to conduct proper onboarding due diligence. Onboarding due diligence is the process of evaluating and assessing the legal risks associated with engaging with a new vendor or supplier before officially establishing a business relationship with them. This process is crucial for organizations to identify potential legal risks and ensure that the vendor's operations are aligned with the organization's own legal and compliance requirements to safeguard the organization from potential financial, operational, reputational, and legal problems that could arise from working with a vendor.

Legal Team Review of Compliance Team Findings

When onboarding a new vendor, the organization's Compliance Team will typically commence the process with a Due Diligence

Questionnaire to gather information from the vendor such as financial health, internal controls, data security protocols, privacy policies, applicable licenses, insurance coverage, compliance with industry laws and regulations, and whether they have been subject to regulatory or civil legal action.

It is not uncommon for the Compliance Team to involve the Legal Team in this process only when they believe there is an issue that warrants escalation. To properly mitigate vendor legal risks, it is important for the Legal Team to carefully review the Compliance Team's findings to proactively mitigate legal risks. This is especially critical for high-risk vendors who pose a greater potential risk to the organization.

By conducting comprehensive onboarding due diligence, organizations can make informed decisions about engaging vendors and manage potential legal risks effectively throughout the vendor relationship lifecycle. This proactive approach helps minimize the chances of disruptions, financial losses, and other adverse consequences that could arise from working with unreliable or non-compliant vendors.

Mitigating Third-Party Vendor Legal Risks

When working with a vendor, there are several legal risks to consider. These risks can vary depending on the nature of the business relationship, the industry involved, and the specific terms and conditions of the contract. Some common legal risks when working with a vendor include:

Contractual Risks:

The contract between your organization and the vendor serves as the foundation for the business relationship. Any ambiguity, inadequate terms, or lack of essential provisions can lead to disputes or misunderstandings. It is crucial to ensure that the contract is clear, comprehensive, and legally sound in the interests of the parties. Key areas to consider:

- **Non-Performance or Breach of Contract:** Vendors might fail to deliver goods or services as agreed upon, leading to a breach of contract. This could result in financial losses, damage to the company's business reputation, and potential legal action to enforce the terms of the contract or seek compensation.

- **Data Security and Privacy:** If a vendor handles sensitive data or customer information on the company's behalf, there is a risk of data breaches or mishandling of personal data. Depending on the jurisdiction and applicable laws, your company could be held liable for any data breaches caused by the vendor.

- **Intellectual Property Infringement:** When working with a vendor, there is a risk that they might infringe on the company's intellectual property rights or use copyrighted material without authorization. This could lead to legal disputes and potential damage to the company's brand and business.

- **Regulatory Compliance:** Vendors may operate in different countries or regions, making it essential to ensure they comply with relevant laws and regulations. If a vendor engages in illegal activities or violates regulations, your company could be implicated as well.

- **Indemnification and Liability:** The contract should clearly outline the responsibilities of each party and include provisions for indemnification, stating who is liable for specific actions or damages. Failure to address these adequately could result in disputes over liability in the case of accidents, injuries, losses, or other incidents.

- **Termination and Exit Strategies:** If the relationship with a vendor sours, or you need to terminate the contract for any reason, it is important to have proper exit strategies and termination clauses in place to avoid legal entanglements.

- **Anti-Competitive Practices:** Some vendors may engage in anti-competitive practices, such as price-fixing or bid rigging, which could expose your company to legal consequences.

- **Risk Mitigation and Contractual Terms:** Based on the vendor legal risk assessment, the organization may implement risk mitigation measures or require the vendor to meet certain compliance standards. Contractual terms should be clear with respect to provisions related to data protection, confidentiality, liability, termination, and dispute resolution.

- **Ongoing Monitoring:** Vendor legal risk management is not a one-time process. Organizations need to con-tinuously monitor vendor conduct throughout the relationship to ensure they remain compliant and meet the agreed-upon standards. Regular assessments and audits may be conducted as part of the ongoing monitoring process.

Know Your Vendors' Vendors:

Vendors often utilize the services of other vendors to provide goods or services on the company's behalf. Part of the vendor onboarding process is to assess your vendors' vendor's operations and activities to ensure you have control over all business activities that can expose your organization to legal risk.

Common Oversight Mistakes Made with Third-Party Vendors:

Many legal and compliance leaders admit that third-party risks were identified after initial onboarding and commencing business relations, suggesting that the compliance and/or legal team's due diligence methods failed to establish proper oversight. Common oversight mistakes to consider:

- **Onboarding Due Diligence Risk Ranking:** When selecting a vendor, a comprehensive due diligence assessment with a vendor risk ranking system should be conducted based on the type and level of service provided by the vendor.

  If you are not risk ranking your vendors, how do you know which vendors bring the most risk to your business and what level of monitoring to implement? A due diligence review can include a review of vendor audited financials, data security and backup systems, continuity and contingency plans, compliance programs, reputation in the industry, and lawsuits or regulatory actions involving the vendor.

- **Contract Renewal Due Diligence:** Vendor due diligence does not end in the onboarding process. Vendor due diligence must continue during the course of the business relationship and at the contract renewal stage.

- **Assuming the Vendor Will Operate in a Legal and Compliant Manner:** Reliance on the vendor to comply with applicable laws and regulations without your ongoing oversight demonstrates a lack of control over the vendor and places your company at serious legal risk.

- **Lack of Clear Contractual Expectations:** Your organization must set clear expectations with respect to the vendor's service performance and contractual expectations. In addition to defining the scope of service, the vendor contract should also contain contract provisions outlining expectations for complying with applicable laws and regulations and contain the right to request information that demonstrates compliance, such as audit and monitoring reports and the right to approve the vendor's use of other vendors. Additionally, the contract should contain provisions for validating data privacy and security and a plan of action for customer complaint response.

- **Inadequate Monitoring of Vendor Activities:** Ongoing monitoring of all vendor activities related to the vendor contract must be conducted to mitigate risks and also to demonstrate your organization's compliance oversight and control over your vendors.

- **Being Prepared for Regulatory Examinations:** Regulatory examiners will request documentation to demonstrate your oversight and control over your company's vendors. Be prepared!

- **Board Oversight:** Keeping the board or committee of the board informed about vendor legal risk management is key to ensuring that they are engaged in vendor risk mitigation and can provide input and/or additional resources to support the program.

Third-party vendor services can provide value and efficiency in their area of expertise. It is important to recognize that when a vendor performs a business activity on the company's behalf, the company can bear ultimate responsibility for potential liability.

The Role of Ethics in Legal Risk Management

While the material in this chapter provides concepts for managing legal risks, it should also encourage ethical behavior. Companies have a duty to obey the law and behave ethically.

Ethics play a significant role in managing legal risk within organizations. Legal risk refers to the potential for legal actions, liabilities, or regulatory penalties arising from non-compliance with laws, regulations, and contractual obligations. Ethics, on the other hand, encompass a set of principles and values that guide individual and collective behavior, focusing on what is morally right or wrong. The role of ethics in managing legal risk can be understood in several ways:

- **Compliance with Laws and Regulations:** Ethical behavior aligns with legal requirements. Organizations that prioritize ethical conduct are more likely to comply with laws and regulations, thereby reducing the likelihood of legal disputes, penalties, and negative consequences.

- **Preventing Unethical Behavior:** Ethical principles guide decision-making and behavior in ways that discourage unethical actions, such as fraud, corruption, or misrepresentation. By fostering a culture of ethical behavior, organizations can minimize the occurrence of activities that could lead to legal troubles.

- **Risk Mitigation:** Ethical behavior often involves risk assessment and mitigation. Organizations that adopt ethical frameworks are more likely to identify potential legal risks early and take proactive measures to prevent or address them. This can include implementing compliance programs, conducting internal audits, and establishing reporting mechanisms for unethical behavior.

- **Stakeholder Trust:** Organizations that prioritize ethics tend to build stronger relationships with stakeholders, including customers, employees, investors, and regulators. Trust is crucial in business interactions and can influence how regulatory authorities and legal systems perceive the organization during legal challenges.

- **Crisis Management:** Ethical organizations are better equipped to handle legal crises effectively. When a legal issue arises, organizations with a strong ethical foundation are more likely to respond transparently, take responsibility for their actions, and work toward resolution. This approach can mitigate reputational damage and potential legal consequences.

- **Legal Defense:** In cases where legal action is taken against an organization, a history of ethical behavior may be used as a defense. Demonstrating a commitment to ethical values can help an organization show that any alleged misconduct was an exception rather than the norm.

In summary, ethics and legal risk management are intertwined. Ethical behavior sets the foundation for legal compliance, risk mitigation, stakeholder trust, and effective crisis management. Organizations that prioritize ethics are more likely to minimize legal risks and create a culture that encourages responsible conduct throughout their operations.

CHAPTER 4
Legal Risk Mitigation Strategy

Legal risk mitigation strategy is a plan to reduce the likelihood and impact of legal risks to an organization. It is an essential part of any company's risk management program. Mismanaging legal risk can have a variety of consequences, including financial loss and reputational harm. There are several different legal risk mitigation strategies that can be used, depending on the specific risks that an organization faces. Some common strategies include:

- **Avoiding the Risk Altogether:** This may be possible by changing the organization's activities or operations. For example, a company that engages in offering risky financial products or questionable healthcare products might avoid the risk of liability by no longer offering those products.

- **Reducing the Likelihood of the Risk:** This can be done by implementing policies and procedures that help to prevent the risk from occurring. For example, a company that offers financial products or healthcare products can implement comprehensive legal oversight to ensure that the products comply with applicable laws and regulations and that customer complaints are monitored and favorably resolved between parties.

- **Minimizing the Impact of the Risk:** This can be done by having a contingency plan in place to deal with the consequences of a risk event, as well as having insurance in place that will provide coverage applicable to the perceived legal risk. For example, a company that is unable to resolve a legal dispute has proper insurance coverage to cover the cost of litigation and potential losses.

- **Transferring the Risk to Another Party:** This can be done by using contracts to shift the responsibility for the risk to another party. For example, a company that imports goods might use a contract with a shipping company to transfer the risk of loss or damage to the goods during transit to the shipping company.

The best legal risk mitigation strategy for an organization will vary depending on the specific risks that the organization faces. However, all organizations should have a plan in place to identify, assess, and mitigate legal risks. This will help to protect the organization from financial loss, reputational damage, and other negative consequences.

Key Points

- **Understand the Business of the Organization:** Legal risk can impact every part of a business, so it is important for legal counsel to have a comprehensive understanding of the business model and objectives when developing a risk mitigation strategy.

- **Keep the Strategy Up to Date:** Legal risks are constantly changing, so it is important to regularly review the risk mitigation strategy and make updates as needed.

- **Communicate the Strategy to Employees:** Employees need to be aware of the legal risks that the organization faces and what they can do to help mitigate those risks.

- **Monitor the Effectiveness of the Strategy:** The risk mitigation strategy should be monitored on a regular basis to ensure that it is effective in reducing legal risks.

Specifically Related Examples of Legal Risk Mitigation Strategies

For a company that is developing a new product or providing a new service:

- Conduct a risk assessment to identify potential legal risks associated with the product or service.

- Consult with experienced legal counsel to ensure that the product or service complies with all applicable laws and regulations.

- Obtain liability insurance to cover the costs of any claims that may arise from the product or service.

For a company that is expanding into a new market:

- Conduct a legal due diligence review of the new market to identify potential legal risks, including geographically related laws and regulations pertaining to contracts, data and consumer privacy, employment, environmental compliance, and more.

- Consult with local legal counsel to advise the company on the laws and regulations of the new market.

- Ensure contracts with local partners comply with local laws, or if specifying a different governing law, that contract provisions can be enforced in the new market jurisdiction.

It is essential for organizations to develop and implement a legal risk mitigation strategy that will help to protect them from financial loss, reputational damage, and other negative consequences. These strategies may include revising contracts, updating policies and procedures, and enhancing employee training.

When It's Too Late

When management meets with legal counsel and asks, "What are our chances we will lose this case, and what would be the potential damages?" it's too late for a preventative legal risk mitigation strategy. Prior to a legal crisis event, the organization needs to be proactive in identifying, managing, and mitigating the possible outcomes from potential events.

For example, when tracking new laws and regulatory developments, legal counsel learned that certain states passed laws prohibiting charging customers a late fee exceeding five dollars and that violation of the law could result in compensatory and punitive damages. An industry publication reported that it was discovered during a government regulatory examination that a competitor of the organization violated this law and had sustained both compensatory and punitive damages, as well as reputational harm. The subject organization quickly evaluated its late fee protocols and learned that it, too, had violated this law by charging a twenty-dollar late fee in the states limiting late fees to five dollars.

Being proactive in tracking new laws and regulatory developments is essential to manage and mitigate potential legal risks. Although the organization in question missed noting the passing of the late fee law limitation, the organization quickly moved to refund the over-charged late fees to customers and subsequently reported the discovered violation as well as the remediation efforts to the regulatory authority. This resulted in a favorable acknowledgment by the regulator, and no further action was taken. Being proactive in monitoring your organization's industry and engaging in corrective action, if necessary, prior to discovery by a regulator is a key legal risk mitigation strategy to minimizing potential negative outcomes.

Risk Mitigation, Not Risk Elimination

Operating with some level of risk is part of running every business, and it's important to accept that not all risks can be eliminated. Eliminating risk means not performing any activity that may carry risk. Such a philosophy would stifle business growth and is an untenable business strategy. The proper strategy is to gain control over the scale and scope of risks inherent in your organization's operations.

Gaining Control of Legal Risks

Gaining control of legal risks is a critical aspect of mitigating legal risks. Strategies to consider in helping to gain control of legal risks:

Smart Contract Drafting

Contracts serve as the foundation for business relationships. Smart contract drafting is essential to mitigate legal risks and ensure that parties' intentions are accurately captured in a legally enforceable document. Some principles and practices to consider when drafting contracts to minimize legal risks:

- **Clear and Precise Language:** Use clear, precise, and unambiguous language to define terms, obligations, and responsibilities.

- **Thoroughly Define Parties and Roles:** Clearly identify all parties involved and their respective roles and responsibilities. This helps prevent confusion and disputes about who is obligated to do what.

- **Detailed Scope of Work or Obligations:** Specify in detail the scope of work, services, or obligations of each party. Avoid broad or vague descriptions that could lead to differing interpretations.

- **Payment Terms:** Clearly define payment terms, including milestones, amounts, and payment methods and schedules. Address late payment penalties and methods of dispute resolution related to payments.

- **Conditions and Contingencies:** Clearly outline any conditions that must be met for the contract to take effect or for certain obligations to be triggered. Consider including contingency plans for unexpected events.

- **Risk Allocation and Liability Limitation:** Clearly allocate risks between the parties and include provisions that limit each party's liability to a reasonable extent. This can help prevent excessive financial exposure.

- **Indemnification and Hold Harmless Clauses:** Include clauses that require one party to indemnify and hold the other harmless for certain types of claims, damages, or losses arising from the contract.

- **Dispute Resolution Mechanisms:** Specify the method of resolving disputes, such as through negotiation, mediation, or arbitration. Clearly outline the procedure to follow if a dispute arises.

- **Governing Law and Jurisdiction:** Clearly state the governing law of the contract and the jurisdiction where disputes will be resolved. This can impact how the contract is interpreted and enforced.

- **Intellectual Property Rights:** Clearly define the ownership and use of intellectual property created or shared under the contract, including any licensing terms.

- **Termination and Exit Strategies:** Clearly outline the conditions and procedures for terminating the contract, including any notice periods and consequences of termination.

- **Confidentiality and Non-Disclosure:** If applicable, include robust confidentiality and non-disclosure provisions to protect sensitive information shared between the parties.

- **Force Majeure and Change Management:** Address unforeseen events (force majeure) and how changes to the contract will be managed.

- **Timeframes and Deadlines:** Clearly specify timelines, milestones, and deadlines to ensure that parties meet their performance obligations in a timely manner.

- **Compliance with Applicable Laws:** Ensure that the contract complies with all relevant laws, regulations, and industry standards.

- **Changes and Amendments:** Specify how changes or amendments to the contract will be handled.

- **Assignment and Subcontracting:** Specify whether the contract can be assigned to a third party or subcontracted. Consider business objectives when allowing or restricting such assignments.

- **Integration:** Clearly state that the contract constitutes the entire understanding and agreement between the parties with respect to the subject matter and supersedes all prior or contemporaneous communications, negotiations, understandings, promises, or agreements, whether oral or written and is intended as a final expression of their agreement.

- **Regular Review of Contract Templates:** Contract templates should be periodically reviewed and updated to reflect changes in circumstances, laws, or regulations that could impact the agreement.

Remember that contract drafting should be tailored to the specific circumstances and needs of the parties involved. It is crucial for legal counsel to ensure that business contracts effectively mitigate legal risks and protect the organization's interests.

Regulatory Review

Regulatory review to mitigate legal risks is a process to assess and ensure compliance with relevant laws, regulations, and industry standards. The goal is to identify potential legal risks and develop strategies to mitigate or minimize them. This process is crucial for avoiding legal disputes, penalties, and reputational damage that can arise from non-compliance with laws and regulations.

- **Product Legal Review:** In addition to an organization-wide regulatory review of compliance with applicable laws and regulations, proactive legal risk mitigation includes legal counsel's review of new products for regulatory and litigation risk before launching the product. Legal counsel should examine the product and applicable laws, benchmark against similar competitor products, and provide a report on potential regulatory violations and lawsuit risks. It is critical to review what may appear as innocuous statements in advertising or on packaging for increased risk of litigation.

- **Documentation:** Maintain thorough documentation of the regulatory review process, including the assessments, action plans, changes implemented, and ongoing monitoring efforts. This documentation can be valuable evidence of your company's commitment to compliance when dealing with government regulatory examinations or in the event of legal challenges.

  By conducting a comprehensive regulatory review and implementing effective mitigation strategies, businesses can reduce legal risks, promote a culture of compliance, and safeguard their operations and reputation.

- **Implement Changes:** Put the mitigation strategies into action by making necessary changes to business operations, policies, and procedures. Ensure that employees are aware of and trained on these changes.

Preemptive Tort Defense

Preemptive tort defense involves taking proactive measures to mitigate potential legal risks and liabilities associated with tort claims. Tort law governs civil wrongs that result in harm or injury to individuals or their property, and preemptive defense strategies aim to minimize the likelihood of such claims arising or to strengthen the defendant's position if a claim does arise.

The liberal use of liability waivers, warning labels, caution signs, safety rails, handguards, and so on can help minimize tort litigation. Liability waivers reduce litigation risk by having individuals specifically agree they will not bring legal action in case of injury during an activity. In other cases, often such litigation turns not on whether someone was injured from a product, but whether they were appropriately warned that such injury could occur. Physical safeguards against injury can help reduce the probability of potential negligence lawsuits by preventing injury in the first place. Businesses that practice prudent preemptive tort defense can lower their legal risks substantially.

Preemptive Tort Defense Strategies to Consider:

- **Risk Management and Prevention:** Identify potential risks and hazards within operations, products, or services and implement measures to prevent harm. This might involve conducting safety assessments, a process or design change, implementing quality control processes, and providing proper warnings and instructions to users.

- **Documentation and Record-Keeping:** Maintain thorough records of your actions, decisions, communications, and safety measures. This documentation can be valuable evidence to demonstrate that you acted responsibly and took steps to avoid the harm alleged in a tort claim.

- **Training and Education:** Provide adequate training and education to employees to ensure they understand and follow proper procedures. Well-trained employees are less likely to make mistakes that could lead to tort claims.

- **Contractual Protections:** Use well-drafted contracts, agreements, and waivers that clearly define responsibilities, limitations, and indemnification clauses. These documents can help allocate risk and protect organizational interests.

- **Compliance with Regulations:** Stay informed about relevant laws, regulations, and industry standards.

Compliance with legal requirements can help to avoid claims related to regulatory violations.

- **Product Liability Prevention:** If your company manufactures or sells products, ensure they meet safety standards and are properly labeled with warnings and instructions for use.

- **Alternative Dispute Resolution (ADR):** Consider including arbitration or mediation clauses in contracts. ADR methods can provide a more efficient and cost-effective way to resolve disputes compared to traditional litigation.

- **Insurance Coverage:** Obtain appropriate insurance coverage to protect against potential tort claims. Liability insurance, such as general liability or professional liability insurance, can help cover legal expenses and potential damages.

- **Legal Experts:** Consult with legal professionals who specialize in tort law to assess potential risks and develop effective preemptive defense strategies.

It's important to note that while preemptive defense strategies can help mitigate legal risks, they may not completely eliminate the possibility of tort claims. If a claim does arise, it's crucial to promptly address it and develop an appropriate response strategy.

Knowing the Law

Taking control of legal risks involves effectively evaluating and understanding the laws and regulations that apply to the business and its specific industry to mitigate potential legal challenges that may arise in various situations. Here are some steps to consider:

- **Identify Applicable Laws:** Understand key laws and regulations that pertain to the industry and nature of the business, which may include local, national, and international laws. Examples include labor laws, environmental regulations, data protection and privacy laws, intellectual property laws, and more. Develop a comprehensive understanding of how applicable laws relate to operations, contracts, business relationships, policies, and other relevant factors to pinpoint areas where legal issues might arise.

- **Stay Informed:** Stay informed and updated on the laws and regulations that apply to your organization's industry and business. New or amended laws and regulations are ongoing, and it's important to stay informed about any developments that might impact the organization.

- **Engage Expert Legal Advice:** Depending on the complexity of the regulatory landscape, consider consulting with legal counsel who specialize in the relevant areas of law. They can provide tailored advice and guidance based on the organization's specific situation.

- **Ethical Considerations:** In addition to knowing the laws and regulations applicable to the organization, it is equally important to ensure the organization operates ethically and transparently. Unethical behavior can lead to serious legal consequences and damage to the organization's reputation.

- **Government and Regulatory Compliance:** Stay informed about government agencies and regulatory bodies that oversee your organization's industry. Adhere to their guidelines and requirements to avoid violations.

Knowing the laws and regulations and how they apply to the organization involves a systematic approach that encompasses the identification, understanding, and implementation of legal oversight measures. Maintaining a proactive stance toward legal risk is essential for avoiding penalties, safeguarding the business's reputation, and ensuring long-term success.

Understanding the Legal Landscape of Data Privacy and Cybersecurity

Understanding the legal landscape of data privacy and cybersecurity involves grasping the various laws, regulations, and frameworks that govern how organizations collect, use, store, and protect personal and sensitive information. This landscape can vary significantly depending on the jurisdiction and the nature of the data being handled. Here are some key aspects and concepts to consider:

- **General Data Protection Regulation (GDPR):** Enforced in the European Union, GDPR is one of the most influential data protection laws. It gives individuals control over their personal data and mandates that organizations handle data responsibly, with clear consent, and appropriate security measures.

- **California Consumer Privacy Act (CCPA):** The CCPA grants California consumers certain rights regarding their personal information and requires businesses meeting certain criteria to be transparent about data collection and sharing practices. In addition to other consumer protection requirements, there are thresholds to fall within the statute's scope to be subject to this law.

- **Colorado Privacy Act (CPA):** The CPA grants Colorado consumers rights with respect to their personal data, including the right to access, delete, and correct their personal data, as well as the right to opt out of the sale of their personal data or its use for targeted advertising or certain kinds of profiling. In addition to other consumer protection requirements, there are thresholds to fall within the statute's scope to be subject to this law.

- **Virginia Consumer Data Protection Act (VCDPA):** The VCDPA gives Virginia consumers the right to access their personal data and request that it be deleted by businesses. It also requires companies to conduct data protection assessments related to processing personal data for targeted advertising and sales purposes. In addition to other consumer protection requirements, there are thresholds to fall within the statute's scope to be subject to this law.

- **Connecticut Data Privacy Act (CTDPA):** The CTDPA contains many similarities to the existing peer legislation in California, Virginia, and Colorado, but it also possesses unique differences. In addition to other consumer protection requirements, there are thresholds to fall within the statute's scope to be subject to this law.

- **Utah Consumer Privacy Act (UCPA):** The UCPA borrows many core elements from peer legislation in California, Virginia, and Colorado but it also possesses unique differences, thus adding to the growing patchwork of state privacy laws that have been forming absent a federal rule. There are thresholds to fall within the statute's scope to be subject to this law.

- It is important to track state law development as there is ongoing activity of additional states introducing new privacy legislation, as well as states that have completed the passage and signing of a new bill with future effective dates.

- **Health Insurance Portability and Accountability Act (HIPAA):** HIPAA applies to healthcare organizations in the United States and sets standards for the security and privacy of patients' medical records and other health-related information.

- **Cybersecurity Frameworks:** Frameworks like the NIST Cybersecurity Framework provide guidelines for organizations to manage and reduce cybersecurity risks. They focus on identifying, protecting, detecting, responding to, and recovering from cybersecurity events.

- **Data Breach Notification Laws:** Many jurisdictions have laws requiring organizations to notify affected individuals and authorities in the event of a data breach that exposes personal information.

- **Financial Sector Regulations:** Financial institutions are subject to regulations like the Payment Card Industry Data Security Standard (PCI DSS) and the Gramm-Leach-Bliley Act (GLBA), which focus on protecting financial data.

- **Sector-Specific Regulations:** Different industries, such as telecommunications, energy, and critical infrastructure, often have specific regulations addressing data privacy and cybersecurity concerns unique to those sectors.

- **International Data Transfers:** Transferring personal data across borders can be subject to specific legal requirements, such as the EU's Standard Contractual Clauses or the EU-US Privacy Shield (prior to its invalidation).

- **Personal Data Protection Bill (India):** India's proposed data protection law aims to establish a comprehensive framework for data protection, consent, and data localization.

- **Government Surveillance Laws:** Some countries have laws allowing government agencies to access data for national security purposes. Examples include the USA PATRIOT Act in the United States and the UK Investigatory Powers Act 2016.

- **Consent and Opt-Out Mechanisms:** Laws often require organizations to obtain informed consent from individuals before collecting or processing their data. Individuals also typically have the right to opt out of certain data processing activities.

- **Data Protection Authorities (DPAs):** Many countries have designated DPAs responsible for enforcing data protection laws, investigating breaches, and providing guidance to organizations.

Understanding the legal landscape involves staying up to date with evolving laws, being aware of jurisdiction-specific nuances, and ensuring compliance to avoid legal penalties and reputational damage. In-house counsel and external legal counsel must possess the knowledge and skills to navigate the cybersecurity landscape effectively.

Responding to Data Breaches

No single federal law or regulation governs the security of all types of sensitive personal information. Determining which federal law, regulation, and guidance is applicable depends in part on the entity or sector that collected the information and the type of information collected and regulated.

The US laws regarding data breach notification require-ments can include but are not limited to the Privacy Act, the Federal Information Security Management Act, the Cyber Incident Reporting for Critical Infrastructure Act of 2022, the Veterans Affairs Information Security Act, the Health Insurance Portability and Accountability Act, the Health Information Technology for Economic and Clinical Health Act, the Gramm-Leach-Bliley Act, the Federal Trade Commission Act, as well as data breach notification laws across all 50 states and US territories. The law applicable to your organization's industry must be assessed to determine if a notification requirement is triggered.

Responding to data breaches and managing legal obliga-tions is a critical aspect of protecting both your organization and the individuals whose data you handle. Here are the general steps to consider in such situations:

1. **Contain the Breach:** As soon as you become aware of a data breach, the first priority is to contain it to pre-vent further unauthorized access or data leakage. This might involve isolating affected systems, disabling compromised accounts, or taking other technical measures to halt the breach.

2. **Assess the Impact:** Determine the extent of the breach and the types of data that have been compromised. This will help you understand the potential risks and take appropriate actions.

3. **Notify Authorities:** Depending on your organization's jurisdiction and the nature of the breach, you may be required to notify relevant regulatory authorities. Laws such as the General Data Protection Regulation (GDPR) in the European Union and the various laws in the United States, such as the Health Insurance Portability and Accountability Act (HIPAA), have spe-cific requirements for reporting data breaches.

4. **Notify Affected Individuals:** In many cases, you will also be legally obligated to inform individuals whose data has been compromised. This notification should be clear and concise and provide information on the breach, the type of data exposed, potential risks, and steps individuals can take to protect themselves.

5. **Legal and Public Relations Teams:** Legal counsel must navigate the legal implications of the breach and provide guidance on addressing potential liabilities. A public relations team should also be involved in managing communication with the media and the public, ensuring that accurate and consistent information is shared.

6. **Implement Remediation Measures:** After containing the breach, it's essential to address the vulnerabilities that allowed the breach to occur. This might involve patching security flaws, updating systems, or enhancing security protocols.

7. **Provide Support to Affected Individuals:** Depending on the nature of the breach, you may need to offer support to affected individuals. This could include credit monitoring services, identity theft protection, or assistance in changing passwords and securing their accounts.

8. **Document Everything:** Maintain a detailed record of the breach, your response actions, and communications with authorities, individuals, and internal stakeholders. This documentation can be crucial for legal and regulatory compliance.

9. **Learn from the Incident:** After the breach has been handled, conduct a thorough post-incident review. Identify what went wrong, what worked well in your response, and what can be improved to prevent future breaches.

10. **Educate and Train:** Data breaches often occur due to human error or lack of awareness. Regularly educate employees about data security best practices and ensure they understand their role in protecting sensitive information.

Remember that your organization's legal obligations can vary based on factors like the type of industry, the countries operating in, and the specific data protection laws that apply. It's crucial to have a well-prepared incident response plan in place that aligns with applicable regulations and involves collaboration between IT, legal, public relations, and management teams.

Gaining Control of Dispute Resolution

Gaining control of dispute resolution involves implementing strategies and practices to actively manage and resolve conflicts and disagreements in a proactive and effective manner. It is helpful to develop a series of steps and strategies aimed at preventing, addressing, and resolving disputes before they escalate and become detrimental to the organization. Consider these steps:

1. **Early Intervention:** Address conflicts as soon as they arise to prevent them from escalating into larger conflicts. Ignoring or delaying resolution can lead to more significant problems down the line.

2. **Alternative Dispute Resolution Methods: Explore various methods such as arbitration and mediation. A neutral** third party can be helpful in facilitating communication between conflicting parties to reach a mutually agreeable solution.

3. **Emotional Intelligence:** Managing emotions is crucial. Emotionally intelligent individuals can recognize and control their emotions, as well as understand and empathize with others' emotions, which aids in resolving disputes.

4. **Legal Understanding:** In situations involving legal disputes, having a full understanding of relevant laws and regulations is essential. This empowers you to make informed decisions and engage in meaningful discussions.

5. **Collaborative Problem-Solving:** When possible, encourage a collaborative approach to resolving disputes where all parties work together to find solutions. Working together promotes a sense of ownership and increases the likelihood of a successful resolution.

6. **Documentation:** Keep accurate records of communications, agreements, negotiation attempts, and actions taken during the dispute resolution process. Documentation helps avoid future misunderstandings and can be crucial in legal or formal settings.

7. **Escalation Pathways:** Establish clear escalation pathways for resolving disputes that cannot be settled through initial efforts. Knowing when and how to escalate a matter to mediation or legal action is important.

8. **Cultural Sensitivity:** Be aware of cultural differences that may impact how disputes are perceived and resolved. Respect diverse perspectives and adapt your approach accordingly.

9. **Maintain Relationships:** Focus on preserving relationships, especially in situations where ongoing business interactions are necessary. A successful resolution should leave all parties feeling respected and valued.

10. **Consistency and Fairness:** Apply consistent and fair principles to dispute resolution, regardless of the nature of the conflict. This builds trust and confidence in the process.

11. **Continuous Improvement:** After resolving a dispute, evaluate the process and outcomes to identify areas for improvement to enhance future resolution strategies.

Dispute resolution is a dynamic process, and there is no one-size-fits-all approach. The key is to approach each situation with patience and a commitment to finding fair and reasonable solutions. By taking control of dispute resolution, you can create a more harmonious and productive environment for all parties involved.

Striking a Balance Between Core Issues and Creative Solutions:

Effective dispute resolution involves addressing the core issue while exploring creative solutions to promote positive outcomes. This can involve:

- **Identifying Core Issues:** Start by clearly defining and addressing the key problems at the heart of the dispute. This establishes a foundation for the resolution process.

- **Openness to Creativity:** While addressing core issues, be prepared to offer creative solutions that may not be immediately apparent. Encourage brainstorming and the exploration of different possibilities.

- **Communication and Understanding:** Foster open communication between parties to ensure that interests and concerns beyond the core issues are understood and considered.

- **Tailoring Solutions:** Craft solutions that directly address the core issues while also considering the broader context and parties' interests.

- **Mediation and Facilitation:** When necessary, engage a neutral third party, such as a mediator, who can guide the process, encourage creative thinking, and facilitate productive discussions.

While it's important to address core issues in dispute resolution, integrating creative solutions can lead to more holistic and satisfying outcomes, fostering better relationships and potentially preventing future conflicts.

Insurance and Risk Transfer Mechanisms in Mitigating Legal Risks

Business insurance represents a form of risk transfer, where financial responsibility for certain legal risks is shifted from the insured party to the insurance company. Business insurance is a critical tool for mitigating legal risks and protecting a company from financial losses that may arise from various legal issues. There are several types of business insurance policies that can help address different legal risks. Here are some common types of business insurance that can help mitigate legal risks:

- **General Liability Insurance:** This type of insurance provides coverage for third-party claims related to bodily injury, property damage, and advertising injuries. It can help protect your business from legal claims arising from accidents that occur on your company premises or due to your business operations.

- **Professional Liability (Errors and Omissions) Insurance:** If your business provides professional services or advice, this insurance can protect you from claims of negligence, errors, or omissions that result in financial harm to your clients.

- **Employment Practices Liability Insurance (EPLI):** EPLI covers claims related to wrongful termination, discrimination, harassment, and other employment-related issues. It helps protect your business against legal actions brought by employees or former employees.

- **Directors and Officers (D&O) Liability Insurance:** D&O insurance is designed to protect company directors and officers from claims alleging mismanagement, breach of fiduciary duty, or other wrongful acts in their roles. However, D&O insurance will not provide coverage for dishonesty, fraud, criminal, or malicious acts committed deliberately. Insurance is created to transfer risk and not to cover the intentional acts of the insured.

- **Cyber Liability Insurance:** In the digital age, businesses face risks related to data breaches, cyberattacks, and privacy violations. Cyber liability insurance can help cover the costs associated with data breaches and other cyber incidents.

- **Product Liability Insurance:** If your business manufactures or sells products, this insurance can protect against claims arising from injuries or property damage caused by company products.

- **Commercial Property Insurance:** This insurance covers damage or loss to business property, including buildings, equipment, and inventory, due to events like fire, theft, or vandalism.

- **Business Interruption Insurance:** This coverage can help replace lost income and cover ongoing expenses if business operations are disrupted due to a covered event, such as a fire or natural disaster.

- **Environmental Liability Insurance: If your business operates in an industry that involves environmental risks, this insurance can provide coverage for cleanup costs and damages resulting from pollution or environmental accidents.**

The Critical Task of Reviewing Insurance Policy Exclusions

Insurance policies are subject to terms, conditions, exclusions, and limits. Not all legal risks may be covered, and legal counsel for the policyholder should carefully review and understand the extent of coverage.

Reviewing insurance exclusions in a business policy is a critical task to ensure that the business has adequate coverage and to understand the limitations of the policy. Exclusions are the specific risks or events that the insurance policy does not cover. Steps to consider in reviewing insurance exclusions in a business policy include:

Read the Policy Document:

Carefully read through the entire policy document. This can be a lengthy and complex document, but understanding its contents is critical. Pay close attention to the following sections:

- **Declarations Page:** This is usually the first page and provides a summary of key policy information, including coverage limits and premium amounts.

- **Insuring Agreement:** This section outlines what the policy covers.

- **Exclusions:** This is the section that lists what the policy does not cover. Exclusions can be specific (e.g., earthquakes) or general (e.g., intentional acts).

- **Conditions:** Conditions outline the terms and requirements you must meet for coverage to be valid.

- **Endorsements/Riders:** These are additional documents that may modify or extend coverage. Be sure to review any endorsements that apply to the policy.

Identify Exclusions:

Highlight or make a list of the exclusions mentioned in the policy. Exclusions can vary widely depending on the type of insurance, so it's essential to be thorough.

Understand the Exclusions:

For each exclusion, understand why it's excluded. The wording can be technical, so if you have any doubts, consider seeking clarification from the insurance agent or consult with other legal counsel knowledgeable in this area.

Evaluate the Company's Needs:

Compare the exclusions to the specific risks and activities of the business. Consider whether any of the exclusions leave the company exposed to risks that are critical to operations.

Consider Optional Coverage:

If you find that some exclusions are concerning and directly related to the organization's business activities, inquire about optional coverage or endorsements that might be available to fill those gaps.

Review and Update Risk Management Strategies:

Insurance exclusions highlight areas where the business may need to improve risk management. If certain risks are excluded, take proactive steps to minimize or mitigate those risks.

Regularly Update the Insurance Policy:

Business needs evolve, so it's essential to periodically review and update the insurance policy to ensure it continues to provide adequate coverage. Remember that understanding insurance exclusions is crucial for making informed decisions about insurance coverage. Failing to do so could lead to unexpected financial losses in the event of a claim.

Legal Risks in Comparative Advertising

Comparative advertising, which involves directly comparing your company's product or service to that of a competitor, can be an effective marketing strategy, but it also carries certain legal risks. These risks can vary depending on the jurisdiction and the specific laws that apply, but some common legal issues associated with comparative advertising include:

- **False Advertising:** Comparative advertising may lead to claims of false or misleading advertising if the comparisons made are not accurate or are intentionally deceptive. If the claims in the advertising are found to be false or misleading, it could result in legal action by competitors or consumer protection agencies.

- **Defamation:** If the comparative advertising includes false statements about a competitor's products or services that harm their reputation, it could lead to a defamation lawsuit.

- **Intellectual Property Violations:** Comparative advertising might involve using a competitor's trademarks, logos, images, or videos without permission. This could potentially lead to a trademark infringement claim as well as legal action for creating confusion among consumers or allegedly damaging a company's reputation.

- **Unfair Competition:** Comparative advertising that is designed to unfairly denigrate a competitor or mislead consumers could be considered unfair competition, which may be prohibited by various laws.

- **Consumer Protection Laws:** There are both federal and state consumer protection laws that prohibit deceptive or misleading advertising practices. Comparative advertising that confuses or misleads consumers could run afoul of these laws.

- **Privacy Violations:** If comparative advertising involves disclosing private information about a competitor or their customers without consent, it could lead to privacy violation claims.

- **Antitrust Law:** In some cases, comparative advertising could raise antitrust law concerns if it is seen as an attempt to unfairly dominate the market or harm competitors.

To minimize these legal risks, businesses engaging in comparative advertising should consider the following steps:

- Ensure that the comparisons made are accurate, verifiable, and supported by objective evidence.

- Avoid making false or misleading statements about competitors.

- Obtain proper authorization to use competitors' trade-marks or copyrighted materials.

- Clearly disclose the source of the comparison and avoid creating confusion among consumers.

- Comply with applicable laws and regulations regarding advertising, trademark usage, and consumer protection.

- Legal counsel must review materials before launching a comparative advertising campaign to assess and mitigate legal risks.

Legal Risk Mitigation with Remote Workers

As work practices transform, so do their associated legal risks. For example, remote work may increase company policy violations, potentially leading to regulatory violations, cyber breaches, litigation, etc. Mitigating legal risks associated with remote workers requires careful planning, clear policies, and effective communication. Here are some steps to consider when addressing potential legal issues related to a remote workforce:

- **Clear Employment Contracts:** Ensure that remote workers have clearly defined employment contracts that outline their roles, responsibilities, compensation, benefits, and any relevant terms and conditions. This will help prevent misunderstandings and disputes.

- **Compliance with Employment Laws:** Remote workers may be subject to different employment laws based on their location. It's important to be aware of and compliant with local labor laws, tax regulations, and other relevant legislation in the jurisdictions where remote workers are based.

- **Data Privacy and Security:** Implement strong data privacy and security measures to protect sensitive company and customer data. Remote workers may access, store, and transmit data from various locations, so having a comprehensive data protection policy is essential. Employers that want to implement surveillance systems for remote workers may be breaching privacy boundaries.

- **Remote Work Policies:** Develop comprehensive remote work policies that cover aspects such as work hours, communication expectations, reporting mechanisms, and performance evaluation criteria. Clearly communicate these policies to remote workers to set expectations.

- **Health and Safety:** Even though remote workers are not physically present at the company, a duty is still owed to ensure their health and safety. Address ergonomic considerations, offer guidance on creating a safe workspace, and provide support if health issues arise due to remote working conditions.

- **Intellectual Property and Confidentiality:** Clearly define intellectual property ownership in employment contracts and establish confidentiality agreements to protect company trade secrets and sensitive information.

- **Communication and Collaboration Tools:** Use secure communication and collaboration tools that comply with relevant security and privacy standards. These tools can help maintain efficient communication while safeguarding sensitive information.

- **Performance Management:** Set clear performance expectations and measurements for remote workers. Regularly communicate with them about their performance, provide feedback, and address any concerns promptly.

- **Anti-Discrimination and Harassment Policies:** Ensure that the company's anti-discrimination and anti-harassment policies extend to remote work situations. Remote workers should feel safe and respected in their work environment.

- **Termination and Exit Procedures:** Develop procedures for terminating remote workers when warranted. This includes addressing issues related to returning company equipment, revoking access to company systems, and ensuring a smooth transition.

- **Worker Classification:** Depending on the jurisdiction, misclassifying remote workers as independent contractors instead of employees can lead to legal trouble. Be sure to properly classify workers according to local labor laws.

- **Insurance Coverage:** Review insurance policies to make sure they cover remote work scenarios, including workers' compensation and liability insurance.

- **Unintentional Bias:** Discrimination can occur if the remote work policy treats employees differently based on protected class characteristics such as age, race, religion, gender, disability, or other characteristics protected by law. Even if the policy is not intended to be discriminatory, disparate impact may occur if employees of a particular group are impacted, such as unintentionally discriminating against women who have childcare responsibilities or workers with disabilities seeking remote work as a reasonable accommodation.

- **Documentation:** Maintain thorough documentation of all interactions, policies, agreements, and performance evaluations with remote workers. This documentation can be crucial in case of disputes or legal challenges.

Legal Risk Tolerance

Legal risk tolerance is a critical concept in business that refers to an organization's willingness and capacity to accept, tolerate, and manage various degrees of risk in pursuit of their business objectives and goals.

Some companies adopt a "zero risk tolerance" policy. However, "zero risk tolerance" does not guarantee zero risk. Believing in zero risk tolerance is counterproductive because it leads to the misallocation of risk management resources and prevents an organization from developing an effective risk mitigation strategy. Legal risk tolerance levels can vary significantly based on factors such as:

- **Industry:** Different industries have varying levels of inherent legal risks. For example, the legal risks associated with a technology startup may differ from those of a healthcare provider.

- **Jurisdiction:** The legal landscape can differ from one jurisdiction to another. Organizations operating internationally need to consider the legal frameworks of multiple countries.

- **Type of Activity:** Certain activities may carry higher legal risks than others. For instance, launching a new product might involve potential intellectual property or product liability risks.

- **Regulatory Environment:** The degree of regulatory oversight and enforcement in a particular sector or region can impact legal risk tolerance.

- **Corporate Culture and Values:** An organization's culture and values can influence how much legal risk it is willing to take on. Some companies may be more risk-averse, while others might embrace risk-taking within certain boundaries.

- **Financial Situation:** The financial strength of an organization can affect its ability to manage legal risks. Smaller companies with limited resources might have a lower risk tolerance.

- **Past Legal Experience:** Previous legal disputes or challenges can shape an entity's future risk tolerance. Organizations that have faced lawsuits in the past might be more cautious.

It's important for organizations to carefully assess their legal risk tolerance and implement risk management strategies, which might include:

- Conducting thorough legal due diligence before entering into contracts or partnerships.

- Consulting with legal counsel experienced in a particular risk scenario to review and advise on important decisions.

- Developing comprehensive compliance programs to ensure adherence to relevant laws and regulations.

- Purchasing insurance coverage to mitigate certain legal risks.

- Establishing clear policies and procedures to guide employees in making legally sound decisions.

Ultimately, determining the appropriate legal risk tolerance level involves careful consideration of the potential benefits and drawbacks of various courses of action while keeping in mind the legal obligations and potential consequences associated with those actions.

Example of Legal Risk Tolerance:

Suppose a ride-share tech startup pushes legal boundaries, such as classifying workers as independent contractors rather than employees, as it attempts to increase market share in a rapidly growing industry. Suppose also that the company was considering whether to expand into a new market in a city that has somewhat hostile regulations for ride-sharing. At the same time, the consequences for entering the market in this city and losing a legal challenge would simply result in either 1) withdrawing from doing business in this city or 2) continuing operating, thereby paying an insubstantial fine and revising the company's business model to comply with the city's regulations. Let's assess the legal risk tolerance level:

- As the new market appears hostile, the likelihood of legal challenges is probably medium or high.

- Relative to the size of the market and potential revenue, a modest fine is a relatively small consequence. We might then classify the severity of outcome impact as low.

- We might classify this company as having an aggressive risk tolerance, since its attitude has been to push the limits to gain market share with a risk-versus-reward business philosophy.

- Although the likelihood of legal action is moderate to high, the potential consequence is low. The decision to enter this new market is likely a low-risk legal decision and within the company's legal risk tolerance level.

Why a Legal Risk Tolerance Strategy Is Important in Business:

- **Decision-Making:** Legal risks are rarely viewed collectively. Different business teams have varying degrees of comfort with risk. For example, sales and marketing teams are willing to take on greater risks to generate new business or "get the deal done" than the legal and compliance teams. How does an organization balance these opposing views? Establishing and understanding the company's legal risk tolerance helps guide decision-making processes. It provides a benchmark for how much risk the company is willing to take on for potential rewards and how conservative or aggressive it should be in establishing business strategies.

- **Strategic Planning:** Identifying the company's risk tolerance is essential for creating a strategic plan that aligns with business goals. For instance, a business with a high-risk tolerance might be more open to exploring new markets, investing in innovative technologies, or pursuing high-growth opportunities. On the other hand, a business with a lower risk tolerance might prefer stable, predictable markets and less volatile strategies.

- **Resource Allocation:** Risk tolerance influences how resources like capital, time, and labor force are allocated within a business. A business with a higher risk tolerance might allocate more resources to research and development, innovation, and aggressive expansion efforts. A business with a lower risk tolerance might prioritize status quo stability.

- **Innovation and Growth:** Businesses with higher risk tolerance are often more willing to embrace innovation and explore new ideas. This can lead to breakthroughs, competitive advantages, and growth opportunities. Conversely, businesses with lower risk tolerance might miss out on potential innovations and growth avenues.

- **Competitive Advantage:** Understanding and managing risk effectively can provide a competitive advantage.

Businesses that accurately assess their risk tolerance can navigate uncertain environments more confidently, allowing them to capitalize on opportunities that their competitors might shy away from.

- **Resilience:** Properly assessing legal risk tolerance helps a business prepare for potential setbacks. By understanding the level of risk they are comfortable with, businesses can develop contingency plans and risk mitigation strategies to minimize potential negative impacts.

- **Investor and Stakeholder Confidence:** Investors, shareholders, lenders, and other stakeholders often evaluate a business's risk profile before getting involved. Demonstrating a clear understanding of risk tolerance and an ability to manage risks can instill confidence in stakeholders and attract investment.

- **Long-Term Viability:** Over time, businesses that consistently align their strategies with their risk tolerance are more likely to have sustainable growth. Pursuing strategies that are too aggressive or too conservative can lead to either missed opportunities or catastrophic failures.

- **Crisis Management:** During times of crisis, businesses with a clear understanding of their risk tolerance are better equipped to respond appropriately. They can make informed decisions about whether to weather the storm, pivot their strategies, or implement immediate changes.

- **Adaptability:** Business environments are constantly evolving, and legal risks can emerge unexpectedly. A business that has a solid understanding of its legal risk tolerance can adapt more quickly to changes, enabling it to remain competitive in dynamic markets.

Can't Just Say No Every Time!

To effectively manage risk, the legal team cannot just say no to new innovations carrying potential risk every time they are asked to evaluate a new product, service or geographical expansion. Legal counsel who cling to the safe space of "no" do not bring any value to the table. The legal team must contribute to the growth and success of the organization by expanding its understanding of new risk areas and business strategies while ensuring alignment with the appropriate level of risk tolerance.

Legal counsel's role should be to help shape business strategies in striking a balance between seizing opportunities and managing potential risk downsides, which is essential for long-term success. The legal team must accept some level of legal risk when the potential business reward warrants it—rather than a consistent "thumbs-down" to new ideas.

Approaching law from a risk mitigation approach is crucial to evaluating the legal environment of business. Evaluating legal risk requires understanding the likelihood of legal action, the severity of the consequences, and the risk tolerance level of the company.

Understanding the organization's legal risk tolerance enables you to take calculated, strategic actions. It is the cornerstone for being bold while being cautious. If you're cautious but not bold, you may never take the necessary risks to achieve the desired business objectives. However, if you're being too bold without taking the time to fully think through the risks of a potential action, you're likely to take too many risks or risks that are too big.

"Well, I don't know as I want a lawyer to tell me what I cannot do. I hire him to tell how to do what I want to do."
-J. P. Morgan

Mitigating Escalated Customer Complaints

Mitigating escalated customer complaints is crucial for businesses to avoid potential lawsuits, minimize regulatory actions, and maintain a positive reputation.

It is not uncommon for organizations to struggle with establishing a policy to define and distinguish between what circumstances constitute a customer inquiry and what factors constitute a customer complaint. Certain types of customer complaints can be defined to be handled directly by designated customer service personnel, whereas any subject matter relating to regulatory issues or a complaint that has been escalated to a regulatory agency, state attorney general, or involves threats of litigation, etc., require the legal team's involvement.

Government regulators use consumer complaints as a trigger for investigating companies, conducting regulatory examinations, and attempting to uncover additional regulatory compliance deficiencies and violations. Typically, a customer service or compliance team member has the responsibility to ensure that customer complaints are addressed responsively. Failing to timely respond to a disgruntled customer can lead to the customer escalating their complaint to a regulatory agency or consumer affairs organization to be heard.

Steps to Consider for Handling Escalated Complaints:

- **Definition of an Escalated Complaint:** Clearly define what constitutes an escalated complaint. It could be a complaint that could not be resolved at the initial stage or a complaint that involves legal or regulatory implications.

- **Designated Escalation Points:** Establish a clear escalation process within the company. Identify specific individuals or teams responsible for handling escalated complaints and the different levels of complaints. This should include members of the legal team, specialized complaint resolution teams, or other relevant personnel.

- **Complaint Handling Process:** Establish a step-by-step process for handling escalated complaints. This may include:

  - **Immediate Acknowledgement:** Ensure that the customer's complaint is acknowledged promptly.

  - **Initial Assessment:** Evaluate the complaint to understand its nature, severity, and potential legal ramifications.

  - **Communication:** Ensure prompt and clear communication with the complainant. Keep the complainant informed throughout the process with regular updates. This can help maintain transparency and build trust.

  - **Investigation:** Conduct a thorough investigation into the complaint, gathering relevant information and evidence to assess the validity of the complaint, support your response, and identify any potential liability for the company.

  - **Collaboration:** Work with other departments (e.g., customer service, quality control) to address the complaint comprehensively.

  - **Resolution:** Determine the appropriate course of action and seek resolution in line with mitigating legal concerns and company policies. Ensure consistency in resolution decisions to mitigate potential future allegations of discriminatory practices.

- **Documentation:** Document everything. Maintain detailed records of all steps taken during the complaint-handling process and all communications with the complainant, including emails, phone calls, and in-person meetings. Accurate documentation can be invaluable if the situation escalates further.

- **Legal Compliance:** Ensure that all actions taken to address the complaint comply with applicable laws, regulations, and company policies. The legal team should review any actions that could have legal implications.

- **Confidentiality and Privacy:** Emphasize the importance of maintaining confidentiality and protecting the privacy of the complainant throughout the process.

- **Timelines and Escalation Procedures:** Set reasonable timelines for each stage of the complaint-handling process to ensure timely resolution.

- **Address Systemic Issues:** If multiple customers raise similar complaints, it may indicate systemic issues within the organization. Addressing these underlying problems can prevent future complaints and potential legal issues.

- **Resolution Options:** If the customer's complaint is valid, offer a fair resolution to rectify the situation and mitigate legal risks. This may involve refunds, discounts, or replacement products or services, depending on the nature and severity of the complaint. Again, ensure consistency in resolution decisions to mitigate potential future allegations of discriminatory practices.

- **Learn from Complaints:** Use customer complaints as an opportunity for growth and improvement. Analyze patterns and trends in complaints to identify areas where the organization can enhance its products, services, or customer support.

- **Training and Support:** Provide training and support to employees involved in handling escalated complaints. This should include guidance on effective communication, conflict resolution, and legal compliance.

- **Reporting and Accountability:** Establish reporting mechanisms to track the number of escalated complaints, their resolution status, and any patterns or trends that may emerge. Hold individuals accountable for their roles in the process.

The above points are just a general framework and specific policies should be tailored to suit the unique needs and requirements of the organization. Legal departments must work in conjunction with other departments to ensure a comprehensive and effective approach to handling escalated complaints.

The Art of Resilience:
Bouncing Back from Legal Risk Setbacks

Bouncing back from legal risk setbacks can be challenging, but with a strategic approach, it is possible to recover and move forward. Here are some steps to consider:

- **Assess the Situation:** Carefully evaluate the nature and severity of the legal risk setback. Identify the key issues and understand the potential short-term and long-term consequences and implications for the organization.

- **Review and Learn:** Conduct a comprehensive review of what led to the legal risk setbacks. Identify any mistakes or weaknesses in your previous approach and learn from them to prevent similar issues in the future.

- **Develop a Recovery Plan:** Senior management and the legal team must create a well-structured recovery plan. This plan should outline the steps you need to take to address the legal issues, mitigate potential damages, and regain control over the situation. This may involve crafting a defense, negotiating settlements, or pursuing alternative dispute resolution methods.

- **Mitigation and Compliance:** Strengthen compliance and risk management practices to prevent future legal setbacks. Review and update internal policies, procedures, and protocols to ensure you're in line with applicable laws and regulations.

- **Open Communication:** Maintain open and transparent communication with stakeholders, including clients, customers, investors, and employees. Address their concerns and keep them informed about the situation, your recovery efforts, and any changes that may affect them.

- **Financial Management:** Assess the financial impact of the setback and make necessary adjustments to allocate sufficient resources to address legal expenses and potential liabilities.

- **Reputation Management:** Protect and rebuild the company's reputation by being honest and proactive in addressing the setback. Focus on delivering quality products or services and emphasize the company's commitment to resolving the issue.

- **Rebuild Relationships:** If the legal risk setbacks have strained relationships with clients, business partners, or other stakeholders, take proactive steps to rebuild trust. Demonstrate the company's commitment to addressing the issues and delivering on its promises.

- **Focus on the Future:** While addressing the current legal challenges is important, don't lose sight of long-term goals. Develop a forward-looking strategy that aligns with business objectives and helps to move past the setbacks.

- **Professional Development:** Treat the setback as a learning opportunity. If the legal risk setbacks were related to a lack of understanding of legal matters, consider investing in your professional development. Gain a better understanding of relevant laws and regulations to avoid similar issues in the future.

- **Stay Committed:** Remember that setbacks are a part of business and life. Stay committed to your goals and stay focused on the steps needed to overcome the legal challenges.

Recovering from legal risk setbacks takes time, effort, and a proactive approach. By addressing the issues head-on, learning from mistakes, and implementing effective strategies, you can work towards a successful recovery and strengthen your company's position moving forward.

CHAPTER 5
The Art of Taking Calculated Legal Risks

Taking calculated legal risks is indeed an art that requires a combination of legal knowledge, strategic thinking, and a clear understanding of the potential outcomes. The law is constantly evolving, and there is no guarantee that a court will rule in your favor, even if you are in the right. This can make it difficult to know when to take calculated legal risks.

Not All Legal Risks Are Created Equal

Not all business legal risks are created equal because they vary in terms of their impact, likelihood, and the degree of control a company has over them. Understanding this differentiation is crucial for effective legal risk management and decision-making within an organization.

Some legal risks are more calculated than others. A calculated legal risk is one that you take after carefully considering the potential benefits and drawbacks. You weigh the odds of success and the potential losses and make a decision based on what you believe is the best course of action. Here are some key considerations for effectively managing uncertainty and taking calculated legal risks:

- **Legal Expertise:** Begin by thoroughly understanding the legal landscape relevant to your situation. Consult with other legal experts who specialize in the relevant area of law to gain insights into potential risks and benefits. Discussing concerns and uncertainties with colleagues can provide fresh perspectives, insights, and potential solutions you might not have considered.

- **Continuous Learning:** Stay updated on legal developments, precedents, and changes in laws and regulations. The more knowledge you have, the better equipped you'll be to address uncertainties and calculated risks.

- **Thorough Research:** When facing uncertain legal issues, dedicate time to comprehensive research. Analyze relevant case law, statutes, regulations, and legal opinions to build a strong foundation for your understanding.

- **Case Analysis:** Break down the legal issue into its constituent parts. Analyze each component separately before attempting to address the issue as a whole. This can help you identify areas where you're more certain and where further research is needed.

- **Be Realistic:** Be realistic about your chances of success. If the odds of success are low, it may not be worth the potential losses. And be prepared for things to go wrong. Even if all the necessary considerations and precautions are taken, there is always the potential for a negative outcome. Be prepared to accept this possibility and have a plan for dealing with the consequences should they arise.

- **Risk Assessment:** Identify and assess the potential legal risks associated with the course of action. Categorize risks based on their likelihood and potential impact. This assessment will help to prioritize and plan accordingly.

- **Scenario Analysis:** Consider different scenarios that could unfold based on your actions. Evaluate how each scenario would impact the organization's goals, finances, reputation, and legal position. This analysis will help prepare for various outcomes and can help you pivot quickly if circumstances demand.

- **Reward Analysis:** Identify and assess potential benefits, gains, or positive outcomes resulting from the decision or action. Consider both short-term and long-term rewards, growth opportunities, etc.

- **Research Precedents:** Research legal precedents, relevant cases, and regulatory decisions that may shed light on how courts or regulatory bodies have interpreted similar situations in the past. This can provide valuable insights into potential outcomes.

- **Ethical Considerations:** When dealing with uncertainty and taking calculated risks, uphold your ethical responsibilities. If you're unsure about a particular course of action, seek guidance on the legal ethics of your plan and consult relevant codes of conduct.

- **Feedback Loop:** Continuously evaluate the outcomes of your decisions and strategies. This can help you refine your approach over time and improve your ability to handle uncertainty effectively.

- **Cost-Benefit Analysis:** Consider the potential costs, benefits, and advantages of taking a particular legal risk. Evaluate whether the potential benefits outweigh the potential downsides and losses.

- **Mitigation Strategies:** Develop strategies to mitigate potential risks. This could involve structuring transactions in a certain way, obtaining necessary permits or approvals, or negotiating contractual terms to minimize exposure.

- **Alternative Paths:** Explore alternative courses of action that might achieve your objectives with lower legal risks. Sometimes, creative solutions can help you achieve your goals while avoiding unnecessary legal challenges.

- **Clear Communication:** Ensure that all stakeholders involved are aware of the potential legal risks and uncertainties. Transparent communication can prevent misunderstandings and conflicts down the line.

- **Contingency Plans:** Develop contingency plans that outline how you'll respond in case certain risks materialize. Having a well-thought-out plan can help you react swiftly and effectively.

- **Regulatory Compliance:** Ensure that your actions are compliant with applicable laws, regulations, and industry standards. Non-compliance can lead to severe legal consequences.

- **Embrace Flexibility:** Recognize that the legal landscape can evolve rapidly. Be open to adjusting your strategies and adapting to new information.

- **Confidence in Core Skills:** Remember that uncertainty doesn't mean you lack legal skills. Trust in your foundational legal education, research abilities, and critical thinking skills.

- **Document Decision-Making:** Keep records of the decisions you make and the rationale behind them. This documentation can serve as a reference for future uncertainties and demonstrate your professional thought process in the event of disputes or legal proceedings.

- **Continuous Monitoring:** Keep a close watch on developments in the legal landscape and any changes in regulations that might impact the situation. This ongoing monitoring helps you adapt your strategy as needed.

Taking calculated legal risks can be a daunting task, but it is often necessary in order to achieve your goals.

Example of a Calculated Legal Risk:

A company is considering entering a new market. The market is highly regulated, and there is a risk that the company's business operations could violate a regulation and the company could be sued. However, the company believes that the potential profits from entering the market outweigh the risks. The company consults legal counsel who assesses the legal risks and develops a legal risk mitigation strategy. After careful consideration, the company decides to enter the market.

In this example, the company took a calculated legal risk. The company weighed the potential benefits and drawbacks, and it decided that the potential profits were worth the risks. Legal counsel also took steps to minimize the risks.

Of course, not all legal risks are calculated. Sometimes, risks are taken without fully understanding the consequences. This can lead to costly mistakes. It is important to always be aware of the risks involved in any legal situation and to make informed decisions.

Case Studies Showcasing Successful Instances of Taking Calculated Legal Risks

Airbnb:

Airbnb's journey to revolutionize the hospitality industry has been paved with calculated legal risks. While not every venture has been smooth sailing, its willingness to challenge the status quo has played a significant role in its success story. Here are some notable examples:

- **Airbnb's User-Generated Content:** Airbnb's platform relies on users listing their properties for short-term rentals. However, this model raised concerns about illegal subletting and violations of local zoning laws. Despite potential legal liabilities, Airbnb expanded rapidly by fostering a community of users and providing tools for hosts to manage risk. Airbnb's approach involved cooperating with governments, implementing host verification processes, and offering insurance coverage to hosts. These calculated legal risks enabled Airbnb to revolutionize the hospitality industry and become a global player.

- **Classifying as a Tech Platform:** Airbnb disrupted the traditional hospitality model operating in the grey area, initially classifying as a tech platform rather than a lodging provider. Taking this calculated legal risk paid off, as Airbnb democratized travel and accommodation, offering unique listings and experiences beyond traditional hotels. It created a global network of hosts and guests, disrupting the industry and capturing a massive market share.

- **Dynamic Pricing Algorithm:** Airbnb's dynamic pricing algorithm, which adjusts prices based on factors like demand and seasonality, drew scrutiny over potential price discrimination and antitrust concerns. Regulators questioned whether it unfairly advantaged hosts in certain locations. Despite legal challenges, the algorithm optimized pricing for both hosts and guests, increasing revenue and booking rates. It provided a more flexible and market-driven approach to pricing, benefitting both parties in the marketplace.

- **Expansion into Untapped Markets:** Entering new regions with complex regulations and cultural sensitivities exposed Airbnb to legal challenges. Taking the calculated legal risk of navigating diverse zoning laws, licensing requirements, and cultural norms presented hurdles in establishing operations. Despite these legal challenges, Airbnb's calculated expansion into untapped markets like China and Cuba diversified its offerings and revenue streams. By adapting to local regulations and partnering with communities, it grew its global presence and user base.

It's important to remember that calculated legal risks can backfire. Airbnb has faced lawsuits, regulatory fines, and public backlash for some of its practices. Nevertheless, its willingness to challenge the status quo and navigate legal complexities has been instrumental in its rise to become a global hospitality powerhouse. Its story offers valuable lessons for businesses seeking to disrupt established industries and achieve success through taking calculated legal risks.

Apple:

Apple has a history of taking calculated legal risks, some with resounding success and others less so. Here are some instances where its boldness paid off:

- **"Think Different" Campaign:** In the late 1990s, Apple was struggling financially and creatively. To revitalize its brand, Apple launched the "Think Different" ad campaign. One of the campaign's ads featured a photo of Mahatma Gandhi, who was known for his nonviolent civil disobedience. However, the Gandhi family held the rights to his image. Apple used the image without permission, risking potential legal action. Ultimately, the Gandhi family decided not to sue, recognizing the positive impact of the campaign and the potential backlash against them. The campaign successfully rebranded Apple as an innovative and forward-thinking company.

- **The App Store's 30% Commission:** When launching the App Store in 2008, Apple imposed a 30% commission on all app purchases and subscriptions. This calculated legal risk raised eyebrows, as it seemed an exorbitant cut compared to competitor platforms like Google Play Store (originally with a 10% commission). Developers and consumers alike cried foul, arguing it inflated app prices and stifled innovation. Apple faced numerous legal challenges, accusations of monopolistic practices, and investigations by international regulators. Despite the backlash, Apple held firm and Apple's App Store became a runaway success. In 2023, the App Store generated over $85 billion in revenue, with developers earning over $230 billion since its launch.

Lessons Learned:

- **Boldness with Calculation:** Apple's willingness to stand firm against initial challenges paid off, but only because its decision was based on a well-defined strategy and value proposition for both developers and users.

- **Investing in Ecosystem:** Apple's 30% commission wasn't solely about profit; it fueled significant reinvestment into the App Store, ultimately benefiting all stakeholders.

- **Adaptability:** While maintaining the core model, Apple adjusted its commission structure in recent years based on app categories and revenue thresholds, showcasing adaptability to evolving market dynamics.

It's important to note that the App Store's success doesn't necessarily justify its commission model on all fronts. Ongoing legal challenges and debates about developer fairness continue. However, these examples exemplify how a calculated legal risk, coupled with a strategic vision and commitment to ecosystem growth, can contribute to remarkable business success.

Netflix:

Netflix's meteoric rise from DVD rental service to global streaming giant wasn't simply built on innovation and content. Throughout its journey, Netflix has embraced calculated legal risks that pushed boundaries and paved the way for its current business success. Here are some notable case study examples:

- **Global Expansion Without Content Licenses:** In the early days of streaming, Netflix aggressively expanded into international markets without securing all necessary content licenses. This exposed it to potential copyright infringement lawsuits and licensing disputes. Despite the legal risks, this rapid global expansion established Netflix as a major player in international streaming markets. It enabled Netflix to gather valuable data on user preferences and content consumption across different regions, laying the groundwork for future content acquisition strategies.

- **Data-Driven Content Recommendations:** Netflix took a calculated legal risk with its recommendation algorithm, which suggests movies and TV shows to users based on their viewing history. This algorithm relies heavily on data analysis of user behavior, which raised allegations of privacy law violations over data collection and potential misuse of personal information.

While the recommendation algorithm was keeping viewers hooked on the platform and contributing to subscriber growth, Netflix implemented strong privacy safeguards and robust data protection measures. The company's willingness to address these concerns head-on allowed it to create a personalized user experience while staying compliant with privacy laws and driving business growth.

- **Independent Content Production:** To address content gaps and secure unique offerings, Netflix made a strategic move to venture into independent film and TV production. This move was a calculated legal risk that challenged Hollywood's traditional production model and raised concerns about potential conflicts of interest with licensing deals. Netflix's investment in original content proved highly successful, generating critically acclaimed hits like *House of Cards* and *Stranger Things*. These shows drew in new subscribers, fostered brand loyalty, and established Netflix as a major content creator, breaking the traditional studio paradigm.

  To mitigate licensing conflicts, Netflix began making direct deals with talent and independent production companies. This allowed for quicker acquisition of new content and avoided contract disputes with traditional studios over licensing revenue.

  Netflix's original content strategy and innovative approach have significantly reshaped the entertainment landscape. Studios are now more open to licensing deals with streaming platforms, recognizing their potential reach and influence. Netflix's success in taking a calculated legal risk has also paved the way for other streaming services to emerge, further diversifying the content landscape and challenging the dominance of traditional studios.

It's important to note that taking calculated legal risks can have downsides. Some of Netflix's ventures resulted in lawsuits, regulatory fines, and public criticism. However, its willingness to test legal boundaries and challenge the status quo has been a significant factor in its journey to becoming a global leader in entertainment. Its case studies offer valuable lessons for businesses looking to disrupt established industries and achieve success through bold but cautious risk-taking.

Tesla:

Tesla has a history of taking bold legal risks in pursuit of its business goals. Here is an example where its calculated legal risk paid off:

- **Tesla's Direct Sales Model:** Tesla's decision to bypass traditional dealerships and sell directly to the consumer through its showrooms was a bold move and calculated risk fraught with legal hurdles and fierce opposition from the established auto industry that aimed to maintain the status quo.

  Tesla actively lobbied for changes in franchise laws, arguing that its direct sales model benefitted consumers by offering transparent pricing, eliminating haggling, and providing a unique brand experience. Tesla invested heavily in online ordering platforms, interactive showrooms, and knowledgeable staff to ensure a smooth and informative buying process for customers, resulting in resounding success.

  Tesla's direct sales model is a prime example of taking calculated legal risks that lead to transformative success. By navigating legal challenges, prioritizing customer experience, and leveraging technology, Tesla secured a competitive edge and disrupted the traditional car dealership model. While legal nuances exist in various regions, Tesla's blueprint and its impact on the industry are undeniable. Tesla's direct sales model stands as a testament to the potential rewards of calculated legal gambles with bold vision and innovative execution.

Uber:

Uber's journey has been paved with calculated legal risks that have, at times, propelled its business but also drawn significant criticism and legal battles. Here are some notable case study examples:

- **Disrupting the Taxi Industry:** In 2012, Uber launched the "Blitz" Strategy, a surprise campaign in San Francisco, flooding the streets with drivers to overwhelm regulators and demonstrate demand. This audacious move, while facing legal challenges, brought massive public attention and solidified Uber's presence in the city.

  From the get-go, Uber's core business model faced legal challenges from traditional taxi companies that argued that Uber operated illegally without proper licensing. Uber took calculated legal risks by pushing its service despite bans and protests, arguing it was a technology platform connecting independent contractors, not a transportation company. This aggressive approach paid off and paved the way for Uber's expansion.

- **Redefining Driver Classification:** Classifying drivers as independent contractors allowed Uber to avoid employee benefits and regulations. This calculated legal risk fueled numerous lawsuits and legislative campaigns advocating for driver rights and benefits.

While challenging in the short term, Uber adjusted its practices in some regions, offering limited benefits and exploring hybrid models that allowed its business to continue its growth.

- **Operating in Unregulated Markets:** Uber entered many cities before regulations were established, forcing local governments to grapple with its new business model. This business strategy, while a calculated legal risk, allowed Uber to gain a foothold and influence the eventual regulations in its favor.

  Uber's disruptive entrance into the transportation industry forced a radical rethink of traditional taxi regulations and labor laws. To achieve its meteoric rise, Uber wasn't afraid to push legal boundaries, taking calculated legal risks that often landed them in courtrooms but ultimately paved the way for its success

Overall, Uber's approach to legal challenges showcases a high-growth tech company's aggressive pursuit of innovation and market dominance, often pushing boundaries before regulations catch up. It's important to note that these examples involve calculated legal risks that paid off in the long run. However, not all calculated risks yield positive outcomes, and companies must carefully evaluate potential legal, financial, and reputational consequences before taking such risks.

Lessons Learned:
Uber's calculated legal risks haven't always paid off. It has faced hefty fines, lost lawsuits, and taken reputational damage. However, its willingness to challenge the status quo has also driven innovation, expanded its market reach, and ultimately contributed to its success.

Uber's case study examples offer valuable lessons for businesses considering taking calculated legal risks:

- **Thorough Risk Assessment:** Carefully evaluate the potential legal, financial, and reputational consequences before taking a risky step.

- **Transparency and Communication:** Be transparent about your intentions and communicate openly with stakeholders, including regulators and the public.

- **Contingency Plans:** Have a plan in place to mitigate potential negative outcomes and adapt to changing legal landscapes.

- **Embrace Innovation:** Taking calculated legal risks can be a powerful tool for driving innovation and disruption, but they should be undertaken with careful consideration and a commitment to responsible business practices.

By understanding the risks and rewards involved, businesses can leverage calculated legal risks to achieve their goals, just like Uber did in its journey to reshape the transportation industry.

It's important to note that these examples involve calculated legal risks that paid off in the long run. However, not all calculated risks yield positive outcomes, and companies must carefully evaluate potential legal, financial, and reputational consequences before taking such risks.

Recognizing When to Take Calculated Legal Risks versus Avoiding Legal Risks Altogether

Recognizing when to take calculated legal risks versus avoiding legal risks altogether is a critical skill for individuals and organizations. Legal risks are inherent in various activities and decisions, and the approach to handling them can vary based on the situation, the potential consequences, and the risk appetite of the organization involved. Consider this framework to help navigate this balance:

- **Importance of the Decision:** Determine how crucial the decision is to the organization's goals. If the decision is central to achieving business objectives, you might be bold in the decision process.

- **Best-Case and Worst-Case Scenarios:** Identify potential legal risks and evaluate the potential outcomes of taking the risk versus avoiding it. What are the best-case and worst-case scenarios? Consider the impact on the organization's reputation, finances, legal liabilities, and other relevant factors.

- **Risk Tolerance:** Understand and discuss the organization's risk tolerance. Some entities are more willing to take on risks for potential gains, while others prioritize avoiding any potential legal entanglements.

- **Legal Landscape:** Understand and evaluate the legal and regulatory environment and whether the decision will potentially run afoul of compliance with applicable laws and regulations.

- **Precedents and Case Law:** Research legal precedents and case law to understand how similar situations have been treated in the past. This can provide insights into how courts and regulatory bodies might view your decision.

- **Ethical Considerations:** Consider the ethical implications of your decision. Sometimes, even if a decision might be legally justifiable, it may not align with your organization's values or societal norms.

- **Contingency Planning:** Have a contingency plan in place in case the risk doesn't pan out as expected. This could involve having exit strategies or a plan B alternative course of action ready.

In some cases, taking calculated legal risks can lead to innovation and competitive advantage, while in others, avoiding risks altogether might be the better course of action. The key is to approach each situation with a clear understanding of the legal landscape, the potential consequences, and your organization's risk tolerance.

Balancing risk and reward is about finding the optimal point where potential gains justify the level of risk taken. It requires careful analysis, strategic thinking, and a willingness to adapt based on changing circumstances. Different situations and contexts will require different approaches, but the fundamental principles of assessing potential benefits against potential consequences remain consistent.

Legal teams are transforming from defenders of the business to also becoming strategic partners. The value they create may be measured by key performance indicators (KPI) that assess how well the legal team helps the organization reduce cost and risk by avoiding litigation and the revenue they help generate by accepting some legal risk when the potential reward warrants it.

Challenging Your Assumptions

Challenging your assumptions is a crucial aspect of taking calculated legal risks. It involves questioning and reevaluating the beliefs, ideas, and biases that you hold in order to gain a deeper understanding of your decisions. Consider this process to follow when challenging your assumptions:

1. **Recognize Your Assumptions:** Start by identifying the assumptions you hold. These are often deeply ingrained beliefs or ideas that you may not even be consciously aware of. Pay attention to your thoughts and reactions in various situations to uncover these assumptions.

2. **Question Your Assumptions:** Once you've identified your assumptions, ask yourself why you hold them. What evidence or experiences led you to believe these things? Are they based on facts, personal experiences, or inherited beliefs? Ask probing questions to get to the root of your assumptions.

3. **Seek Contradictory Information:** Actively seek out information, perspectives, or experiences that challenge your assumptions. This could involve reading articles or books from different viewpoints and engaging in respectful debates with others to see things differently and broaden your perspective.

4. **Engage in Self-Reflection:** Spend time reflecting on your assumptions and how they impact your thoughts, behaviors, and decisions. Consider whether your assumptions still hold true in light of new information or experiences. Be open to the possibility that your assumptions may need revision.

5. **Experiment and Test:** Challenge your assumptions by experimenting with new behaviors, beliefs, or ideas. Test your assumptions in real-world situations to see if they hold up or if there's room for adjustment.

6. **Stay Humble and Open-Minded:** Recognize that everyone has assumptions, and no one has a complete monopoly on truth. Cultivate an open mind and a willingness to admit when you might be wrong or when your assumptions need to change.

7. **Learn from Mistakes:** Don't be afraid to admit when your assumptions are mistaken or incomplete. Embrace these moments as opportunities for learning and growth.

8. **Regularly Review Your Assumptions:** Make it a habit to periodically review and challenge your assumptions. As you gather new information and experiences, your

beliefs may evolve, and it's important to stay adaptable and open to change.

Challenging your assumptions can be uncomfortable, as it may require you to confront your biases and rethink long-held beliefs. However, it's a valuable process that can lead to greater self-awareness and improved decision-making when taking calculated legal risks.

Separating Sense and Nonsense

Balancing legal risks with business strategies is an intricate practice that organizations must perform to navigate the complex landscape of the corporate world. However, this process is not without its challenges, as it often involves distinguishing between what makes legal sense and what might seem like nonsense.

Nonsense in decision-making can manifest in various ways, leading to suboptimal choices and outcomes. This phenomenon often arises from cognitive biases, irrational thinking, or the influence of irrelevant factors. Here are some aspects of nonsense in decision-making:

Cognitive Biases:

- **Confirmation Bias:** People tend to favor information that confirms their preexisting beliefs or values, ignoring contradictory evidence. This can lead to decisions based on incomplete or skewed information.

- **Overconfidence Bias:** Individuals may overestimate their own abilities or the accuracy of their judgments, leading to decisions that are overly optimistic and not grounded in reality.

- **Anchoring Bias:** Decisions can be swayed by the initial information received, even if it is irrelevant or arbitrary. The first piece of information becomes the "anchor," influencing subsequent judgments.

Emotional Decision-Making:

- **Fear and Anxiety:** High-stress situations can lead to decisions driven by fear or anxiety rather than rational analysis. This may result in impulsive choices that do not consider long-term consequences.

- **Elation and Euphoria:** Conversely, positive emotions can cloud judgment, leading to overly optimistic decisions without a thorough evaluation of risks.

Groupthink:

Group decision-making may suffer from conformity and a desire for harmony within the group, suppressing dissenting opinions. This can lead to decisions that lack critical scrutiny and diverse perspectives.

Influence of External Factors:

Decisions can be influenced by irrelevant external factors, such as the presentation of information, who presents it, or the framing of choices. The way a decision is presented and by whom can significantly impact the outcome.

Lack of Information:

Making decisions with insufficient or inaccurate information can lead to nonsensical outcomes. Incomplete data or a lack of understanding can contribute to poor decision-making.

Failure to Learn from Experience:

Individuals may repeat the same mistakes if they fail to learn from past experiences. This reluctance to adapt and evolve can perpetuate nonsense in decision-making.

Addressing nonsense in decision-making requires awareness of these pitfalls and a commitment to employing rational and evidence-based approaches. Encouraging critical thinking, fostering a culture of openness to diverse perspectives, and promoting continuous learning can help mitigate the impact of irrational decision-making.

Distinguishing between sense and nonsense in the realm of legal risks often revolves around the understanding and interpretation of laws, regulations, and contractual agreements. Sensible decision-making requires a nuanced understanding of the legal framework within which a company operates, coupled with a strategic vision that ensures growth and sustainability while nonsense arises when companies neglect legal guidance, employ irrational decision-making, or overreact to improbable scenarios.

In a world where decisions shape our collective destiny, the ability to call out nonsense in decision-making is a formidable tool. It is a commitment to reason, evidence, and accountability. The most successful businesses are those that foster a culture that values critical thinking and open dialogue where individuals can contribute to a more robust decision-making process, ensuring that the choices made today pave the way for a prosperous future.

CHAPTER 6
Business Startups

Startups are new companies with high growth potential that enter the market with a bold strategy of industry disruption and scaling up. However, the vision of disruption and growth for a business startup often comes with increased legal risk that can be perilous for startups. Balancing legal risks with ambitious growth strategies is crucial for long-term success. Failing to address legal risks early on can lead to significant setbacks or even business failure.

Characteristics of Business Startups

Promising Aspects

- **Investor Interest:** Investors are often attracted to startups with ambitious growth plans as they envision higher returns on their investments. This can result in increased funding opportunities.

- **Market Expansion:** Aggressive growth strategies usually involve expanding into new markets, reaching a wider customer base, and potentially dominating a niche. This can lead to increased revenue and brand recognition.

- **Competitive Advantage:** Being the first or fastest mover in a market can give a startup a competitive edge, allowing them to capture significant market share before competitors enter.

- **Talent Attraction:** Ambitious startups often attract top-tier talent who are excited about the opportunity to be a part of a high-growth venture.

Challenging Aspects

- **Regulatory and Compliance Challenges:** Operating in new markets or rapidly expanding can expose the business to a complex landscape of regulatory and compliance requirements. Non-compliance can lead to legal penalties and reputational damage.

- **Intellectual Property Concerns:** Expanding too quickly might lead to overlooking proper intellectual property protection, potentially resulting in legal disputes over patents, trademarks, copyrights, etc. Startups often rely heavily on intellectual property (IP) to differentiate themselves from competitors. However, without proper IP protection, they might face infringement claims or lose their competitive advantage.

- **Contractual Obligations:** Rapid growth could strain the startup's ability to fulfill contractual obligations, leading to breach of contracts and potential legal actions. Startups enter into various agreements, such as partnerships, vendor contracts, employment agreements, and client contracts. If these agreements are not properly drafted, they could lead to negative legal consequences.

- **Employee and Labor Issues:** Hiring at a fast pace can lead to labor law violations, improper classification of employees, and potential legal disputes related to labor practices, including wage and hour violations, workplace safety regulations, and potential discrimination or harassment claims.

- **Data Privacy and Security:** Entering new markets might involve handling customer data that is subject to different data protection laws, potentially leading to data breaches, privacy violations, regulatory actions, and other legal consequences.

- **Lawsuits and Litigation:** Aggressive competition and expansion can increase the likelihood of disputes and lawsuits from competitors, customers, or other sources.

- **Financial Risks:** Rapid growth can strain the startup's finances, leading to cash flow issues, potential bankruptcy, and legal actions from creditors.

- **Securities Law Violations:** If startups seek external funding, they need to adhere to securities laws that regulate fundraising activities. Failing to comply with these laws can lead to legal penalties and reputational damage.

- **Product Liability:** If a startup's product causes harm to customers, it could result in product liability claims. Ensuring the safety and quality of products is essential to mitigate this risk.

- **Disputes with Cofounders or Partners:** Disagreements among cofounders or business partners can lead to legal battles over ownership, intellectual property rights, and decision-making authority.

- **Tax Issues:** Startups must navigate complex tax laws, including income tax, sales tax, and potentially international tax considerations if they operate in multiple jurisdictions.

- **Environmental Regulations:** Depending on the nature of the startup's business, they might need to comply with environmental regulations, especially if their operations involve waste, emissions, or hazardous materials.

Mitigation Strategies

- **Legal Counsel's Role:** The role of legal counsel is to guide the startup through properly structuring the business entity to limit personal liability, address compliance requirements, licensing requirements, intellectual property protection, strong contracts, and other legal aspects. It is important for legal counsel advising startups to have an entrepreneurial spirit.

- **Due Diligence:** Thoroughly research and understand the legal and regulatory landscape of new markets before entering them.

- **Risk Assessment:** Conduct regular risk assessments to identify potential legal pitfalls and implement strategies to mitigate them.

- **Proactive Compliance:** Invest in building a strong company culture of compliance from the outset to minimize legal risks.

- **IP Protection:** Ensure proper Intellectual Property (IP) protection of innovations.

- **Insurance Coverage:** Consider obtaining appropriate insurance coverage to mitigate financial risks arising from legal challenges.

Business startups can indeed attract high legal risks, primarily due to their vulnerable nature, limited resources, and the complex regulatory environment in which they may operate. While startups may face higher legal risks compared to established businesses, balancing ambitious expansion plans with prudent legal strategies can mitigate these risks and increase the chances of long-term success.

Crypto Startups

Lawyers advising crypto startups will need to navigate the complex and rapidly evolving legal landscape of the cryptocurrency and blockchain industry. Here are some key considerations and critical areas:

- **Regulatory Compliance:** Cryptocurrencies and tokens often fall under different regulatory categories depending on their use and features. Stay up to date with the regulatory environment in your jurisdiction and others where your clients operate. This includes securities laws, anti-money laundering (AML) regulations, and know-your-customer (KYC) requirements.

- **Token Classification:** Determine whether the tokens your clients are creating or using are classified as securities, utility tokens, or payment tokens. This classification will impact how they are regulated and the legal requirements they must adhere to. In the U.S., the SEC believes that almost all tokens are considered securities, and therefore must comply with existing SEC regulations, and that only a digital currency like Bitcoin can be considered a commodity that falls outside the SEC's jurisdiction. Therefore, it is crucial that token issuers consider the regulatory implications of offering a token before launching.

- **Security Laws:** If the tokens are deemed securities, they will be subject to securities laws. Help your clients understand and comply with regulations such as the Securities Act of 1933 (in the United States) and other securities laws.

- **AML and KYC:** Assist your clients in implementing Anti-Money Laundering (AML) and Know Your

Customer (KYC) procedures to prevent illegal activities like money laundering and fraud. This may involve identity verification processes for token holders and transaction monitoring.

- **Licensing and Registration:** Some jurisdictions require crypto-related businesses to obtain licenses or registrations to operate legally. Help your clients navigate these requirements and obtain the necessary approvals.

- **Data Privacy:** Blockchain technology often involves the processing of personal data. Ensure that your clients are compliant with data protection laws such as the General Data Protection Regulation (GDPR) if they process personal information.

- **Smart Contracts and Code Audits:** A smart contract, like any contract, establishes the terms of the agreement. But unlike a traditional paper contract, a smart contract's terms are executed as code running on a blockchain platform such as Ethereum and automatically execute, control, or document events and actions according to the terms of a contract. Review and advise on the smart contracts developed by your clients to ensure they are legally sound and minimize potential vulnerabilities. Code audits can help identify security risks.

- **Intellectual Property:** Advise on intellectual property strategies to protect your clients' innovations, including patents, trademarks, and copyrights related to their blockchain or crypto projects.

- **Consumer Protection:** Help your clients draft user agreements and terms of service that are clear, fair, and compliant with consumer protection laws. This includes providing accurate information about risks associated with cryptocurrencies.

- **Fundraising and Token Sales:** If your clients are conducting Initial Coin Offerings (ICOs) or Security Token Offerings (STOs), guide them through the legal aspects of fundraising, including drafting offering documents and ensuring compliance with relevant regulations.

- **Cross-Border Considerations:** Cryptocurrencies and blockchain projects often cross international boundaries. Understand the legal implications of operating in multiple jurisdictions and help your clients navigate cross-border challenges.

- **Litigation and Dispute Resolution:** In the event of disputes or legal challenges, provide representation and advice to help your clients navigate legal proceedings effectively.

- **Collaboration with Regulators:** Establish lines of communication with regulatory authorities to stay informed about potential changes in regulations and to foster a cooperative relationship.

- **Education and Training:** Educate your clients about the legal and regulatory implications of their actions in the crypto space. Empower them to make informed decisions.

Given the complexity of the crypto and blockchain industry, it's crucial to stay updated on new developments, regulations, and best practices, and even engage in inquiries and open communication with regulators to ensure comprehensive advice for your clients.

Six Key Questions When Operating in the Blockchain Space

Operating in the blockchain space requires navigating a myriad of regulatory requirements that can vary by jurisdiction. Crypto products and tokens may differ depending on the organization and the offering, but here are six key questions that should be addressed when launching a crypto startup.

1. **Will there be advertising to the public?** If a company advertises to the public, anti-fraud and consumer protection laws come into play. Regulators in the US from the Federal Trade Commission (FTC) and the Consumer Financial Protection Bureau (CFPB), together with state attorneys general, have oversight and enforcement of the laws, rules, and regulations involving advertisements to the public. If the product is classified as a security, the US Securities and Exchange Commission (SEC) will have oversight of advertising. Statements, promotional materials, etc., will be scrutinized to ensure they do not contain statements or promises that are false, misleading, or deceptive. Legal counsel must be involved in the marketing development process and review all promotional statements and materials before publishing them.

2. **Would a person reasonably rely on company statements believing they will profit from their purchase?** Blockchain companies issuing tokens or blockchain-based assets may have to comply with securities laws.

   The test determining whether a token is an "investment contract" and subject to securities laws is the **Howey Test.** The Howey Test is a legal framework used in the United States to determine whether a particular transaction qualifies as an "investment contract" and, therefore, falls under the definition of a security.

The Howey Test derives its name from the 1946 US Supreme Court case "SEC v. W.J. Howey Co." (SEC v. W. J. Howey Co., 328 US 293, 66 S. Ct. 1100, 90 L. Ed. 1244, 163 A.L.R. 1043, May 27, 1946), which set the precedent for how securities laws should be applied to certain investment arrangements. It has been widely applied in various contexts, including traditional securities and, more recently, in determining whether certain offerings or transactions involving cryptocurrencies and blockchain-based assets fall under securities regulations.

It's important to note that the Howey Test is not a formal law or statute; rather, it's a legal precedent that has evolved through case law. Courts consider its principles to determine whether a particular transaction should be categorized as an investment contract and thus be subject to securities regulations.

In the context of blockchain and cryptocurrencies, the Howey Test has gained significant attention due to its implications for determining whether certain tokens or offerings qualify as securities. The application of the Howey Test to various blockchain projects and token sales has been the subject of ongoing debate and regulatory scrutiny. This is because many blockchain-based projects issue tokens that may have attributes of both utility and investment, making it challenging to determine whether they should be regulated as securities. Regulators, including the US Securities and Exchange Commission (SEC), have been grappling with how to classify and regulate various tokens and blockchain-based projects. As blockchain and cryptocurrency and its applications continue to evolve, so does the discussion around the Howey Test and its applicability to the blockchain industry.

The debate primarily revolves around whether certain tokens are sufficiently decentralized and have utility beyond just serving as investment vehicles. Tokens that have clear utility within a functional network, where they are necessary for accessing or interacting with a specific platform or service, might be considered more likely to pass the Howey Test as non-securities. On the other hand, tokens that are marketed as investments with an expectation of profits and are closely tied to the efforts of a central entity could be deemed securities. The Howey Test consists of four key criteria:

1. **Investment of Money:** There must be an investment of money or value, which could be in the form of traditional currency, cryptocurrency, or other valuable assets.

2. **Common Enterprise:** The investors' money must be pooled with the expectation of profits being derived primarily from the efforts of others. In other words, investors are relying on the efforts and expertise of a third party, typically the issuer or a promoter, to generate profits.

3. **Expectation of Profit:** Investors must have a reasonable expectation of profit from their investment. This profit expectation is usually tied to the efforts of the third party, as mentioned earlier.

4. **Efforts of Others:** The profits must come predominantly from the efforts of others, namely the issuer or its agents. This criterion is the linchpin of the Howey Test, as it helps distinguish between a security and other forms of investments.

    In the context of blockchain and cryptocurrencies, the application of the Howey Test has become crucial to determine whether a token sale, initial coin offering (ICO), or any other token-related transaction falls under securities regulations. If the token or digital asset meets the criteria of the Howey Test, it is likely to be considered a security, and the issuer would be subject to relevant securities laws and regulations enforced by the US Securities and Exchange Commission (SEC).

5. **Will the company transmit a person's money?** Blockchain companies acting as "administrators" or "exchangers" of "convertible virtual currency" (CVC) may be considered to be money transmitters by federal regulators. Pursuant to federal regulations, as well as regulations in most states, if a company has the authority or power to issue, remove, or exchange a cryptocurrency or virtual currency, the company may be required to register as a "money services business" under the federal Bank Secrecy Act (BSA), which requires companies to assist the US Government in detecting and preventing money laundering. Additionally, 49 states also have money transmission laws. In addition to reviewing applicable federal law, it is equally important to conduct a state-by-state analysis to determine the states in which the company should obtain a money transmission license.

6. **Will employees have access to material, non-public information?** If a company's employees will have access to material, non-public information such as pricing of the company's publicly traded digital asset or any other asset trading on a platform controlled by the company, the company must develop employee insider trading training and implement and enforce insider trading policies to prevent employees, consultants, or other insiders from profiting on material, non-public information.

7. **Will the company collect and store consumer data?**
Collecting and storing consumer data is subject to
various federal and state privacy laws and regulations,
such as the General Data Protection Regulation (GDPR)
in the EU and the California Consumer Privacy Act
(CCPA). Colorado, Connecticut, Utah, and Virginia have
passed similar privacy laws, with additional states in
the process of following suit. Privacy laws can vary by
jurisdiction and require the company to clearly communicate its data collection practices through privacy
notices, as well as inform consumers of their rights to
data accessibility and the right to deletion under certain circumstances. Compliant data security protocols
are critical to comply with regulatory requirements
and to prevent data breaches.

8. **Where will the product or token be launched?**
Companies should be aware of sanctions programs
in the jurisdictions in which they plan to operate. In
the US, the Office of Foreign Assets Control (OFAC)
enforces compliance with US sanctions programs.
Conducting transactions with sanctioned persons or
in a sanctioned jurisdiction is an offense, and OFAC
may impose penalties on a "strict liability standard."
This means that OFAC can hold violators civilly liable
regardless of whether they knew they participated in
a transaction with a sanctioned person or entity. It
is critical to have OFAC policies and internal controls
(e.g., customer screening and IP address blocking)
intended to prevent prohibited transactions.

These six questions are not exhaustive but are key to
developing a legal risk mitigation strategy when starting a
blockchain company.

Legal risks are a major concern for all businesses, but they

can be especially daunting for startups. It is especially important that legal counsel participate early on when making
decisions about business structure, intellectual property protection, employment law, contracts, regulatory and licensing
requirements, and overall potential liability. Balancing legal
risks with business strategies is essential in mitigating legal
challenges while supporting long-term success.

FinTech Startups

FinTech startups can face various legal risks that need to be
carefully considered and managed. Here are some common
legal risks to consider with FinTech startups:

- **Regulatory Compliance:** FinTech startups often operate in heavily regulated industries, such as finance,
  payments, and lending. They need to comply with
  numerous financial regulations, including but not
  limited to the Equal Credit Opportunity Act (ECOA),
  the Truth in Lending Act (TILA), data protection and
  privacy laws, Anti-Money Laundering (AML) laws,
  and Know-Your-Customer (KYC) regulations. Failure
  to comply with these regulations can result in hefty
  fines and legal penalties.

- **Licensing and Permits:** Depending on the nature of
  the FinTech business, specific licenses or permits to
  operate legally may be required. For instance, payment
  processors might require money transmitter licenses,
  and lending platforms might need consumer lending
  licenses. Operating without the necessary licenses can
  lead to serious legal consequences.

- **Intellectual Property:** Protecting intellectual property
  (IP) is crucial in FinTech, especially if the startup

has developed innovative technologies or software. This could include patents for unique algorithms or software, trademarks for branding, and trade secrets. Failure to protect IP can lead to disputes and loss of competitive advantage.

- **Contractual Agreements:** FinTech startups frequently enter into partnerships, collaborations, and agreements with other businesses, financial institutions, and technology providers. Poorly drafted contracts, misunderstandings, or breaches of contract can lead to legal disputes.

- **Data Privacy and Security:** FinTech companies handle sensitive financial and personal data. A breach of data privacy or inadequate security measures could result in legal actions from customers and regulatory bodies.

- **Anti-Money Laundering (AML) and Fraud:** FinTech businesses need to have robust systems to detect and prevent money laundering, fraud, and other financial crimes. Failure to do so can result in regulatory fines and reputational damage.

- **Marketplace Regulations:** If the FinTech startup operates in a marketplace connecting borrowers and lenders or buyers and sellers, it might face legal issues related to transparency, fairness, and, in many cases, need to satisfy state licensing requirements.

- **Cross-Border Operations:** If the FinTech startup operates internationally, navigating the legal and regulatory landscapes of multiple jurisdictions is critical. This can involve complex compliance challenges and potential conflicts of laws.

- **Consumer Complaints and Disputes:** Dissatisfied customers or clients might raise complaints or initiate legal actions against the FinTech startup. Having clear dispute-resolution mechanisms and customer support processes can help mitigate these risks.

To manage these legal risks effectively, legal counsel should have expertise in financial regulations, technology law, data privacy, and other relevant areas. Additionally, implementing strong internal compliance measures, conducting regular risk assessments, and staying up to date with evolving regulations are essential for maintaining legal compliance and minimizing potential legal issues.

CHAPTER 7
International Expansion and Cross-Border Transactions

Expanding internationally and engaging in cross-border transactions can offer significant growth opportunities for businesses, but they also come with a range of legal risks and challenges because they involve the laws of multiple jurisdictions. There are also legal risks related to the enforcement of contracts and judgments. It's important to thoroughly understand and address these risks to ensure a successful expansion.

Key Legal Considerations

- **Compliance with Foreign Laws:** Different countries have varying laws and regulations governing advertising, consumer protection, data privacy, employment, and more. Ensure that marketing materials, including advertisements, promotions, and product claims, comply with the specific regulations of each target market and that labor laws are being followed. Failing to comply with local laws can lead to fines, legal disputes, or even business shutdowns.

- **Cultural and Language Differences:** What works in one culture might not be suitable or could even be offensive in another. Cultural nuances, local customs, and sensitivities need to be considered to avoid unintended negative reactions that could harm the organization's brand reputation. Misunderstandings due to language differences can lead to communication breakdowns, contract disputes, and overall operational difficulties.

- **Intellectual Property Protection:** Protecting intellectual property (IP) across borders can be complex. Trademarks, copyrights, patents, and trade secrets may be subject to different rules and enforcement mechanisms in different countries. It is critical to understand each country's IP laws and process for possibly registering the company's IP rights in each relevant jurisdiction.

- **Foreign Investment Laws:** Some countries have restrictions on foreign investment in certain industries or require approval for foreign-owned businesses. Understanding these laws and obtaining necessary permissions is vital.

- **Contractual Agreements:** International contracts should be carefully drafted to address potential disputes related to jurisdiction, choice of law, and methods of dispute resolution. Enforcing contracts across borders can be challenging. International contracts might be subject to international trade laws, such as the United Nations Convention on Contracts for the International Sale of Goods (CISG).

- **Currency and Exchange Controls:** Dealing with foreign currencies and managing exchange rate risks can affect financial performance. Be aware of countries that have strict controls on currency exchange and repatriation of profits.

- **Political and Economic Instability:** Unforeseen political changes, economic downturns, and social unrest in foreign markets can disrupt business operations and investments.

- **Import/Export Regulations:** Cross-border transactions involve import and export regulations, customs duties, tariffs, and trade barriers. Non-compliance can result in delays, fines, or confiscation of goods.

- **Labor Laws and Employment Regulations:** Hiring employees abroad comes with complying with various labor laws and employment regulations in foreign markets, including employment contracts, minimum wages, workplace conditions, and termination procedures.

- **Sanctions and Export Controls:** Be knowledgeable of international trade sanctions and export control regulations that restrict trade with certain countries. The Office of Foreign Assets Control (OFAC) of the US Department of the Treasury administers and enforces economic and trade sanctions based on US foreign policy against targeted foreign countries and regimes, terrorists, international narcotics traffickers, those engaged in weapons of mass destruction, and other threats to national security. Conducting transactions with sanctioned persons or in a sanctioned jurisdiction is an offense, and OFAC may impose penalties on a "strict liability standard." This means that OFAC can hold violators civilly liable regardless of whether they knew they participated in a transaction with a sanctioned person or entity. It is critical to have OFAC policies and internal controls (e.g., customer screening and IP address blocking) intended to prevent prohibited transactions. Implement robust screening processes to check individuals, entities, and transactions against sanctions lists, as well as educate employees about potential red flags and the consequences of non-compliance.

- **Data Privacy and Security:** Collecting, storing, and processing personal data across borders requires adherence to various data protection laws, such as the EU's General Data Protection Regulation (GDPR).

- **Taxation and Transfer Pricing:** Managing taxes across different jurisdictions requires an understanding of international tax treaties, transfer pricing rules, and potential double taxation issues.

- **Local Partnerships and Joint Ventures:** Collaborating with local partners or entering joint ventures may help gain local market knowledge but might expose the business to risks associated with partner actions, local laws, and cultural differences.

- **Disputes:** A dispute with a business partner or customer in a foreign country can be difficult and expensive to resolve because of the legal system in different countries.

- **Anti-Corruption and Anti-Bribery Laws:** International business transactions can expose an organization to incidents of bribery and corruption. Businesses must ensure compliance with anti-corruption laws like the Foreign Corrupt Practices Act (FCPA). The FCPA prohibits bribing foreign officials and imposes strict penalties.

The Foreign Corrupt Practices Act (FCPA) is a United States federal law that addresses issues of bribery and corruption in international business transactions. Enacted in 1977, the FCPA has two main components: the anti-bribery provisions and the accounting provisions.

1. **Anti-Bribery Provisions:** The FCPA's anti-bribery provisions prohibit the bribery of foreign officials to obtain or retain business. It applies to individuals and companies subject to US jurisdiction, including foreign companies that are listed on US stock exchanges or conduct business in the US. This part of the FCPA makes it illegal to offer, pay, promise, or authorize payments or anything of value to foreign officials or government representatives in order to obtain or retain business or gain an unfair advantage.

2. **Accounting Provisions:** The accounting provisions of the FCPA require companies to maintain accurate books and records and to have internal controls in place to prevent and detect financial wrongdoing, including bribery and corruption. These provisions are designed to ensure transparency and accountability in financial transactions and to prevent companies from disguising illegal payments as legitimate business expenses.

   The FCPA has been an important tool in the fight against global corruption and has had a significant impact on international business practices. It has helped promote a more level playing field for companies operating internationally and has encouraged higher standards of ethics and compliance.

   In addition to the FCPA, there are other anti-bribery laws and international conventions that address similar issues, such as the United Kingdom's Bribery Act, the OECD Anti-Bribery Convention, and the United Nations Convention against Corruption. These laws and conventions work together to combat bribery and corruption on a global scale, fostering fair and transparent business practices.

Companies operating internationally should be aware of the applicable laws and regulations to ensure they remain compliant and uphold ethical standards in their business dealings. Violations of anti-bribery laws can result in severe penalties, including fines and criminal prosecution for individuals and companies involved in corrupt practices. It's advisable for companies to establish strong anti-corruption compliance programs and conduct thorough due diligence when entering into international business transactions.

Steps to Consider to Mitigate These Legal Risks

- Conduct thorough legal and regulatory research before entering a new market.

- Consult with local legal experts and advisors who understand the specific legal landscape of the target country.

- Develop a comprehensive risk management strategy that includes legal, financial, and operational aspects.

- Implement strong internal compliance programs to ensure adherence to relevant laws and regulations.

- Draft clear and comprehensive contracts that address potential disputes and challenges.

- Stay informed about political, economic, and legal developments in the target country.

Remember that the legal risks associated with international expansion and cross-border transactions can vary greatly depending on the specific countries and industries involved. It's essential to approach each new market with careful planning and due diligence.

Think Corporate Responsibility when Tempted to Cross the Line

International business and corruption are two interconnected topics that often intersect in the global economic landscape. Corruption can manifest in various forms, such as bribery, embezzlement, and extortion. When it comes to international business, corruption can have significant implications for companies. Here's a closer look at the relationship between international business and corruption:

- **Business Environment:** Corruption can create an unpredictable and uneven playing field for international businesses. Companies might be forced to engage in corrupt practices to secure contracts, permits, or favorable regulatory treatment, thus distorting fair competition. Act responsibly and resist!

- **Market Entry:** In some countries, corrupt practices might be a common way of doing business. Companies entering such markets may face pressure to engage in corrupt practices themselves to navigate bureaucratic hurdles or gain access to essential resources. Act responsibly and resist!

- **Legal and Regulatory Risks:** Engaging in corrupt activities can lead to legal consequences, including fines and reputational damage. Many countries have laws, such as the US Foreign Corrupt Practices Act (FCPA) and the UK Bribery Act, that prohibit companies from bribing foreign officials.

- **Reputation:** Companies associated with corruption can suffer severe damage to their reputation, which may impact customer loyalty, investor confidence, and employee morale.

- **Company Ethics:** Companies that make corporate ethics part of its policies and practices understand corporate responsibility in business practices and might be less willing to engage with corrupt partners.

- **Economic Development:** Corruption can hinder economic growth by diverting resources away from productive activities, discouraging foreign investment, and undermining the rule of law.

- **Global Supply Chains:** Corruption within supply chains can result in substandard products, unsafe working conditions, and violations of labor rights, impacting the reputation and legal liability of international companies.

- **Due Diligence:** Companies conducting business internationally are increasingly expected to conduct thorough due diligence to identify and mitigate corruption risks. This includes assessing the integrity of partners, understanding local legal and cultural contexts, and implementing robust compliance programs.

To address the challenges posed by corruption in international business, various initiatives and organizations promote transparency, ethical conduct, and accountability. For instance, the United Nations Global Compact encourages companies to adopt sustainable and socially responsible practices, and Transparency International works to raise awareness about corruption and advocate for anti-corruption measures.

Overall, the relationship between international business and corruption underscores the importance of ethical behavior, responsible business practices, and international cooperation to create a fair and equitable global economic landscape.

CHAPTER 8
Emerging Trends and Future Legal Risks

The legal landscape is constantly evolving, and lawyers representing organizations, whether in-house counsel or external legal counsel, need to be prepared to adapt to new trends and future legal risks.

Future Legal Trends

Anticipating future legal trends requires an understanding of current trends and potential developments in various areas of law. Here are some legal trends to consider:

- **The Growing Complexity of Regulations:** Businesses are facing an increasing number of regulations, and lawyers need to be up to date on the latest requirements. This can be a challenge, as regulations are constantly changing. Stay updated by actively tracking laws applicable to the organization's industry, as well as new court decisions. Follow government agency websites applicable to the organization's industry. Subscribe to industry publications and attend industry events and conferences to learn the latest trends.

- **The Increasing Importance of Legal Technology:** Legal technology is rapidly evolving, and lawyers need to be familiar with the latest tools and technologies.

These tools can provide better efficiency and productivity.

- **The Demand for Lawyers with Business Acumen:** Corporate lawyers have typically focused on providing reactive legal services, such as contract enforcement, regulatory action, and litigation resolution. However, the role of corporate lawyers is shifting to being more proactive and acting as strategic advisors. Corporate counsel must have a strong understanding of the company's business and industry to effectively advise their clients while exploring opportunities for growth. Thinking strategically is key to helping clients balance legal risks with business strategies to achieve their business goals.

Future Legal Challenges

Anticipating future legal challenges requires an understanding of potential developments in various areas of law. General areas where legal challenges may be encountered in the future:

- **Data Privacy and Cybersecurity:** As technology continues to advance, data privacy regulations are likely to become more complex and stringent. Corporate lawyers will need to navigate evolving data protection laws, such as the General Data Protection Regulation (GDPR), the California Consumer Privacy Act (CCPA), and the many additional states that have already enacted similar privacy laws or are in the legislative process, while also addressing emerging issues related to data breaches and cybersecurity.

- **Artificial Intelligence (AI) and Automation:** With the increasing use of AI and automation in various industries, legal challenges related to intellectual property, liability for AI-generated content, and both ethical and regulatory concerns about biased algorithms are likely to arise. Government regulators are already focused on biased algorithms related to consumer finance.

- **ESG Consideration:** Businesses are increasingly being held accountable for their environmental, social, and governance (ESG) practices. In recent years, ESG factors have gained prominence as investors and stakeholders started focusing on this issue. This is leading to new legal risks, such as potential lawsuits for environmental damages and allegations of discrimination. Corporate counsel need to be aware of ESG risks and navigate the legal implications to mitigate them.

- **Blockchain and Cryptocurrency:** The legal landscape for blockchain technology and cryptocurrencies is rapidly evolving. Corporate lawyers may face challenges related to regulatory compliance, initial coin offerings (ICOs), smart contracts, and disputes involving blockchain-based transactions.

- **Antitrust and Competition Law:** As technology giants continue to expand their influence, antitrust and competition law challenges are likely to emerge. Corporate lawyers may need to address issues related to market dominance, monopolistic practices, and the impact of emerging technologies on market competition.

- **Remote Work and Labor Law:** The widespread adoption of remote work arrangements could lead to legal challenges related to employment contracts, labor law compliance, and worker classification (employee versus independent contractor). Corporate lawyers will need to navigate these issues to ensure businesses are compliant with applicable regulations.

- **Supply Chain and Global Trade:** Global supply chains are susceptible to disruptions due to geopolitical tensions, natural disasters, and pandemics. Corporate lawyers will need to assist companies in managing these risks, ensuring compliance with international trade regulations, and addressing potential disputes.

- **Intellectual Property in the Digital Age:** As content creation and distribution methods evolve in the digital era, corporate lawyers will need to address intellectual property challenges in areas such as digital media, streaming services, and online platforms. Issues related to copyright, trademark, and patent protection could arise.

- **Healthcare and Biotechnology:** Advances in biotechnology and healthcare innovation can lead to legal challenges around intellectual property rights, regulatory approvals, and ethical considerations. Corporate lawyers working in these industries will need to stay updated on the evolving legal landscape.

- **Crisis Management and Reputation Protection:** Companies may face various crises that require legal expertise to manage effectively. These crises could include public relations disasters, product recalls, or ethical misconduct. Corporate lawyers will play a crucial role in advising companies on how to protect their reputations and navigate legal implications.

To prepare for these future challenges, corporate lawyers should stay informed about legal developments and develop a deep understanding of the industries in which their clients operate. Adapting to technological advancements and embracing interdisciplinary collaboration will also be essential for addressing emerging legal challenges.

Overall, the evolving role of corporate counsel involves a shift from being purely legal advisors to becoming integral members of the business team, contributing to strategic decision-making, and fostering a culture of legal and ethical compliance within the organization.

Legal Risks with Artificial Intelligence—Can Too Much Data Lead to Biased Lending Decisions?

Lenders are increasingly relying on artificial intelligence (AI), machine learning, and other digital technologies to determine credit eligibility. Regulators are increasingly taking notice of how companies use AI, especially as it applies to perpetuating unlawful discrimination and bias in data. There is a concern that discriminatory lending practices involving AI can occur due to unintentional biases present in the data used to train AI models and in the design of algorithms. Because AI and big data make it possible to integrate large-scale information containing a greater number of data factors than ever before, does it open the door to factoring in too much data, thus creating the potential for bias? AI models learn from the input of historical data, and if certain variables are added to the mix or are given more weight than others, AI decision-making may reflect unfair and discriminatory practices.

There are strong reasons to believe that with the use of large-scale information, AI will naturally rely on proxies in its decision-making that can discriminate on the basis of age, race, or gender. Proxies are characteristics or data points that are not directly related to age, race or gender, but can be used to make inferences or guesses about it. For example, whether someone owns a Mac or PC, or their type of phone, tablet, etc., can be indicators of a person's credit repayment patterns, but can also be indicators of a person's age, race or gender. These protected class attributes may also be derived from email domain preferences, such as whether the loan applicant uses

Gmail, Hotmail, or an AOL account, etc., from which data on payment performance can also be associated. Protected class attributes can also be associated with the types of store credit accounts reported on the applicant's credit history. Although such data can be correlated to loan repayment patterns, it is also a proxy for age, race, and gender. Assigning certain types of retail store credit accounts a weighted factor can have disparate impact effects. What about the time of day? AI may decide that submitting a loan application at 2 A.M. may be a sign of financial desperation when it's nothing more than an applicant who works the night shift. What if the applicant's credit report shows numerous medical bills? Although paid current, AI may extrapolate medical bills to mean that the health of the applicant is in question, and therefore, they are not a good credit risk, resulting in credit denial or less affordable loan terms. Then, there is the scrutiny of first and last name and zip code, resulting in potential discriminatory connections. With the goal of creating greater access to credit, AI could be programmed to assess many nontraditional supplemental factors for borrowers who do not have a strong credit history. Could the use of expanded data factors have the opposite effect by resulting in discriminatory credit denials or less attractive lending terms?

Given the opportunity to input an unlimited number of factors into the AI model under the belief that more data is better may result in a snowball effect akin to the problems credit scoring models experienced in the beginning with the overuse of data factors and continue to struggle with accusations of bias. Just because there is a possible statistical relationship does not mean that it is predictive of anything.

When it comes down to it, is more data truly needed to make a predictive credit decision beyond factors such as credit history, income stability and ability to repay? Is there any doubt that AI credit decisions, just like credit scoring models, will result in credit applications being denied that may have been justifiably approved using a smaller window into the credit applicant's soul?

FinTech, MedTech, Now LegalTech

Just as FinTech revolutionized the financial industry and MedTech transformed healthcare, LegalTech is making its mark on the legal sector.

The emergence of LegalTech, short for "legal technology," refers to the growing intersection of technology and the legal industry. Like FinTech and MedTech, LegalTech encompasses a wide range of tools, software, platforms, and innovations that aim to streamline, improve, and transform various aspects of the legal field. LegalTech has gained significant traction in recent years due to advancements in technology and the increasing demand for more efficient and cost-effective legal services. Here's a brief overview of each:

FinTech (Financial Technology)

FinTech refers to the integration of technology into financial services and processes. It aims to enhance financial transactions, improve access to financial services, and create innovative solutions for traditional banking and investing. FinTech encompasses online banking, mobile payment apps, robo-advisors, blockchain-based solutions, and peer-to-peer lending platforms. Some key trends in FinTech include:

- **Digital Payments:** The adoption of mobile wallets, contactless payments, and cryptocurrency for every-day transactions.

- **Blockchain and Cryptocurrency:** The growth of block-chain technology and the mainstream adoption of cryptocurrencies like Bitcoin and Ethereum.

- **Neobanks:** Digital-only banks that don't have any physical branches.

- **InsurTech:** Refers to the use of technology innovations designed to find cost savings and efficiency from the current insurance industry model.

MedTech (Medical Technology)

MedTech involves the application of technology to healthcare and medicine. This can include devices, software, and processes that enhance patient care, diagnosis, treatment, and research. Recent developments in MedTech include:

- **Telemedicine:** The widespread adoption of remote healthcare services, allowing patients to consult with doctors virtually.

- **Health Wearables:** Wearable devices that track and monitor health metrics, such as heart rate, sleep patterns, and activity levels.

- **Personalized Medicine:** Tailoring medical treatments to individual patients based on their genetic makeup and other factors.

- **AI in Healthcare:** Applying artificial intelligence to analyze medical data, assist in diagnoses, and predict disease outcomes.

- **Robotics in Surgery:** The use of robotic systems to assist surgeons in performing complex procedures with higher precision.

- **Electronic Health Records (EHR) Systems:** Ensuring the privacy and security of patient health data in an increasingly digital healthcare landscape.

LegalTech (Legal Technology)

LegalTech involves the application of technology to the legal industry to simplify and improve legal processes. It can encompass tools and software that assist with legal research, contract management, electronic discovery, document automation, and virtual law firms. LegalTech aims to increase efficiency, reduce costs, and enhance collaboration within the legal profession. LegalTech has been evolving rapidly, with developments like:

- **E-Discovery:** The use of technology to identify, collect, and analyze electronic information during legal proceedings.

- **AI in Law:** Leveraging artificial intelligence to automate contract review, legal research, and predictive analytics for case outcomes.

- **Blockchain in Legal:** Implementing blockchain technology for secure and transparent contract management and property transactions.

- **Regulatory Compliance:** Tools that help businesses stay compliant with changing regulations and mitigate legal risks.

- **Online Dispute Resolution:** Digital platforms that facilitate the resolution of disputes without the need for traditional court proceedings.

- **Predictive Analytics:** Predictive analytics use historical data, court decisions, regulatory actions, and dispositions to forecast potential legal outcomes, which can aid in litigation strategy decision-making.

- **Virtual Law Firms:** Virtual law firms operate entirely or partially online, leveraging technology to provide legal services remotely and efficiently.

These three tech sectors are all experiencing significant growth and innovation, driven by a combination of technological advancements, shifting consumer expectations, and regulatory changes. The ongoing convergence of technology and these industries is likely to continue shaping the way financial, medical, and legal services are provided in the years to come.

The benefits of LegalTech include increased efficiency, reduced costs, improved accuracy, enhanced access to legal services, and the ability to utilize technology to mitigate legal risks. However, the adoption of LegalTech also presents challenges related to data security, legal ethics, and the potential displacement of some traditional legal roles.

Staying aware of emerging legal trends is crucial for businesses and legal teams. The legal landscape is constantly evolving due to changes in technology, society, and global events. By being aware of these trends, corporate counsel can help their companies to balance legal risks with business strategies.

Staying Ahead of the Curve: The Forward-Thinking Lawyer

Staying ahead of the curve on future trends is essential for lawyers to provide effective and relevant legal services to their clients. Here are some tips to consider for staying informed and prepared:

- **Continuous Learning:** Commit to lifelong learning. Attend seminars, workshops, webinars, and conferences to stay updated on legal developments and emerging trends in your practice area. Online platforms and legal publications can also provide valuable insights.

- **Technology Proficiency:** Embrace technology in your practice. Stay informed about legal tech tools, AI-powered research platforms, and software that can streamline tasks like document review, case management, and research.

- **Networking:** Build a strong professional network. Engage with colleagues, mentors, clients, and other professionals in your industry. Join bar associations, legal forums, and online communities to exchange ideas and insights.

- **Industry Knowledge:** Understand your clients' industries. This will help you anticipate legal issues and challenges they might face in the future. Regularly read industry publications and reports to stay informed.

- **Strategic Thinking:** Develop strategic thinking skills. Analyze trends in law, economics, politics, and technology to anticipate how they might impact your practice area and clients.

- **Scenario Planning:** Imagine potential future scenarios and their legal implications. This foresight can help you prepare strategies and legal solutions in advance.

- **Collaboration:** Collaborate with professionals from different disciplines. Cross-disciplinary insights can provide a broader perspective on emerging trends that could affect your practice.

- **Client Education:** Educate your clients about potential legal changes that could affect their businesses. By positioning yourself as an informed and proactive advisor, you can build stronger client relationships.

- **Thought Leadership:** Write articles and blog posts or give presentations on emerging legal issues. Establish yourself as a thought leader in your practice area, which can enhance your reputation and credibility.

- **Global Awareness:** Be mindful of international developments. Many legal trends are influenced by global events, so staying informed about international legal, economic, and political changes can be valuable.

- **Ethical Considerations:** Stay updated on ethical guidelines and considerations related to emerging technologies and trends. Ethical dilemmas may arise from new practices or innovations, so being prepared is crucial.

- **Adaptability:** Cultivate adaptability and a willingness to embrace change. The legal landscape is continually evolving, and lawyers who can adapt quickly will thrive.

- **Macro Trends:** Stay aware and up to date on macro trends like climate change, cybersecurity, data privacy, and social justice issues. These trends often generate new legal challenges and opportunities.

- **Predictive Analytics:** Explore tools and techniques that utilize data and predictive analytics to anticipate legal trends. These insights can help you make more informed decisions.

- **Mentorship and Reverse Mentorship:** Mentorship can provide experience-based insights, while reverse mentorship from new colleagues can offer fresh perspectives on technology and emerging trends.

Staying ahead of the curve requires dedication and consistent effort. By embracing change, staying curious, and actively seeking new knowledge, you can position yourself as a forward-thinking lawyer who provides exceptional value to your clients.

CHAPTER 9
Leveraging Legal Risks for Competitive Advantage

Leveraging legal risks for competitive advantage is a concept that involves a strategic approach to managing legal challenges and regulatory uncertainties in a way that benefits a business. While the idea might sound counterintuitive at first, it essentially involves turning potential legal liabilities into opportunities that can enhance a company's position in the marketplace. However, it is important to note that leveraging legal uncertainties or regulatory gaps to gain a competitive edge over rivals requires careful consideration and ethical conduct, as improper actions can lead to severe consequences, both in terms of reputation and legal repercussions.

Here are some considerations to keep in mind when exploring the concept of leveraging legal risks for competitive advantage:

- **Identify Legal Risks:** Begin by thoroughly identifying and assessing potential legal risks that the business may face. This could include regulatory compliance issues, intellectual property disputes, product liability concerns, environmental regulations, data privacy issues, and more.

- **Innovative Solutions:** Instead of merely avoiding or mitigating legal risks, look for innovative ways to address them that can give an organization a competitive edge. This might involve finding novel approaches to comply with regulations while also offering unique value to customers.

- **Regulatory Sandboxes:** In some jurisdictions, government agencies provide regulatory sandboxes that allow companies to test innovative products or services without specific regulations to see if innovative ideas can benefit the public and enter the market. The point is to allow these businesses to "play" in the sandbox without the typical regulatory restrictions. This can be an opportunity to develop and refine unique offerings that meet compliance standards.

- **Market Niche:** If you identify a legal gray area or an underserved market due to regulatory constraints, consider whether you can operate in that space ethically and legally. Being an early mover in such areas can provide a competitive advantage if regulations evolve favorably.

- **Adaptation and Agility:** Maintain a flexible approach to adapt to changing legal landscapes. Regulations can change rapidly, and being agile in adjusting your strategies can help you capitalize on shifting legal dynamics.

- **Public Relations and Branding:** How you navigate legal risks can have a significant impact on the organization's brand reputation. Being transparent about efforts to comply with laws, adopting ethical practices, and demonstrating a commitment to responsible business conduct can attract customers who value integrity.

- **Risk Management Expertise:** Consider collaborating with legal experts or consultants who specialize in risk management and regulatory affairs. Their insights can help you navigate complex legal landscapes more effectively and perhaps make changes to achieve a competitive advantage.

- **Ethical Considerations:** While leveraging legal risks can offer competitive advantages, it's crucial to ensure your actions remain within ethical boundaries. Avoid engaging in unethical behavior, exploiting legal loopholes in harmful ways, or intentionally violating laws for short-term gains.

- **Long-Term Strategy:** When leveraging legal risks, think about the long-term sustainability of your approach. Short-term gains that compromise corporate integrity or expose the organization to significant legal liabilities can ultimately harm the business in the long run.

- **Continuous Monitoring:** Stay vigilant about changes in laws and regulations that affect the organization's industry. Regularly reassess your strategies to ensure they remain compliant and aligned with business objectives.

Leveraging legal risks for competitive advantage requires a delicate balance between innovation, ethical conduct, and strategic thinking. It's essential to approach this concept with caution, transparency, and a commitment to responsible business practices. When done right, leveraging legal risks can help an organization stand out in the marketplace while maintaining its integrity and reputation.

A Complex and Ethically Sensitive Strategy

Leveraging legal risks for competitive advantage is a complex and ethically sensitive strategy that involves leveraging legal uncertainties or regulatory gaps to gain a competitive advantage. While it may seem like an attractive option for businesses seeking an edge, it's important to continue to note that this approach can have significant negative consequences, both in terms of reputation and legal repercussions. Here are some points to consider:

Advantages:

- **First-Mover Advantage:** If a company is willing to take calculated risks in uncharted legal territories, it might gain a first-mover advantage, establishing itself as a leader in a new market or business model.

- **Cost Savings:** By pushing the boundaries of existing regulations, a company might find ways to reduce costs or streamline processes, giving it a cost advantage over competitors.

- **Market Differentiation:** Embracing innovative legal strategies can set a company apart from its competitors and attract customers who are drawn to its unique approach.

Risks and Ethical Concerns:

- **Reputation Damage:** Operating in a legal gray area or using questionable tactics can tarnish a company's reputation, leading to negative public perception and decreased customer trust.

- **Legal Consequences:** Exploiting legal risks could result in legal actions, fines, penalties, and even criminal charges. These outcomes can outweigh any short-term competitive gains.

- **Uncertainty:** Legal landscapes are unpredictable, and exploiting legal ambiguities can backfire if laws change or regulatory bodies crack down on previously tolerated practices.

- **Ethical Implications:** Pursuing competitive advantage through legal risks may violate ethical standards, making it difficult to attract and retain employees, customers, and investors who prioritize responsible business practices.

- **Long-Term Viability:** Relying on a strategy built on exploiting legal risks might not be sustainable in the long run, especially as regulations become more robust and transparent over time.

While leveraging legal risks for competitive advantage might seem tempting, it's important to carefully consider the potential consequences. A more sustainable and responsible approach is to find that competitive edge through ethical business practices, compliance with regulations, and innovation within legal boundaries. This approach can help build a strong foundation for long-term success while minimizing the risks associated with exploiting legal uncertainties.

Examples of Leveraging Legal Risks for Competitive Advantage

Leveraging legal risks for competitive advantage is a complex and potentially controversial strategy. Companies must be cautious when employing such tactics, as they can lead to negative consequences, damage to reputation, and result in serious legal difficulties. However, there have been situations where companies have strategically navigated legal risks to gain an edge. Here are a few examples:

- **Ride-Sharing Platforms:** Ride-sharing companies initially operated in a regulatory gray area, challenging traditional taxi regulations as they entered new markets by exploiting regulatory loopholes or challenging existing regulations. They leveraged legal risks to gain a competitive advantage through offering lower prices resulting from lower operational costs made possible due to not having to comply with local taxi regulations. They also established a presence in certain markets before traditional taxi companies or regulators could react.

- **Tech Companies and Data Privacy:** Some technology companies have been accused of exploiting legal ambiguities related to data privacy and user consent to collect and utilize user data for targeted advertising and other purposes. While taking this calculated legal risk to obtain a competitive advantage has led to legal challenges and public backlash, it has also allowed these companies to generate significant revenue from personalized advertising as well as achieve sustainable growth.

- **Pharmaceutical Industry:** Brand-name pharmaceutical companies sometimes challenge drug manufacturers' generic version of a drug, even when the validity of an existing patent is in question. This can lead to legal battles that delay the entry of generic versions into the market, extending the brand-name company's monopoly period and maintaining higher prices for their drugs.

- **Cryptocurrencies:** The emergence of cryptocurrencies and initial coin offerings (ICOs) introduced legal ambiguities. Some companies leveraged this uncertainty to raise funds quickly before regulators could clarify their stance.

It's important to note that while these examples illustrate instances where companies have attempted to leverage legal risks for competitive advantage, these strategies can come with significant legal, and reputational challenges, and especially raise ethical concerns. In many cases, companies engaging in such practices face criticism, legal action, and potential damage to their long-term viability and reputation. It is advisable for companies to prioritize ethical business practices, legal compliance, and maintain a positive public image while working to achieve a competitive edge.

CHAPTER 10
Next-Generation Legal Teams

The evolving role of corporate legal teams, whether in-house or external counsel, has been undergoing significant evolution in response to the rapidly changing business landscape. As businesses face new challenges and opportunities, legal counsel must adapt and expand their roles to provide effective legal guidance and support. Here are some key aspects of the evolving role of corporate legal counsel that can shape next-generation legal teams:

- **Strategic Business Partner:** Corporate counsel are no longer seen solely as legal advisors; they are now essential strategic partners to the executive team. They actively participate in business discussions and decisions, offering legal insights to help shape business strategies while ensuring compliance with laws and regulations.

- **Risk Management and Compliance:** In today's complex regulatory environment, corporate counsel play a pivotal role in identifying and mitigating risks. They develop and implement compliance programs to ensure that the company operates within legal boundaries, avoiding costly litigation and regulatory penalties.

- **Innovation and Technology:** As technology continues to advance, corporate counsel are responsible for navigating legal challenges related to data privacy, intellectual property, and emerging technologies such as artificial intelligence and blockchain. They help the company harness the benefits of technology while staying compliant and protecting sensitive information.

- **Globalization and Cross-Border Operations:** Many businesses now operate on a global scale, which introduces a host of legal and regulatory considerations. Corporate counsel must have a strong understanding of international laws, trade agreements, and cultural differences to guide their companies through international expansions and transactions.

- **Environmental and Social Responsibility:** There's a growing emphasis on corporate social responsibility and environmental sustainability. Corporate counsel are often involved in ensuring the company's operations align with environmental regulations and ethical practices, which can contribute to reputation management and long-term business success.

- **Mergers and Acquisitions:** Corporate counsel are instrumental in facilitating mergers, acquisitions, joint ventures, and other business transactions. They conduct due diligence, negotiate terms, and ensure legal compliance throughout the process.

- **Employment and Labor Law:** The changing nature of work, including remote work arrangements and the gig economy, brings forth new legal challenges. Corporate counsel advise on employment contracts, workplace policies, and labor law compliance to foster a productive and legally sound work environment.

- **Crisis Management:** In the event of a crisis, such as a data breach or a product recall, corporate counsel work closely with public relations and management teams to address legal implications and protect the company's reputation.

- **Ethics and Governance:** Corporate counsel often play a critical role in maintaining strong corporate governance and ethical standards. They advise boards of directors on matters of corporate ethics, transparency, and compliance.

- **Interdisciplinary Skills:** The evolving role of corporate counsel demands a broader skill set. They need to be not only excellent lawyers but also effective communicators, strategic thinkers, and business-minded professionals who can collaborate across the organization.

- **Adaptability and Continuous Learning:** As the business world continues to change rapidly, corporate counsel must remain adaptable and committed to ongoing learning. Staying informed about legal and industry developments is crucial to providing relevant and effective guidance.

Legal counsel will no longer be confined to a narrow legal role. As pivotal players, legal counsel will help shape a company's strategic direction, manage risks, and ensure compliance in a complex and dynamic business landscape. Adopting the ability to combine legal expertise with business acumen makes legal counsel an indispensable asset to modern organizations.

Anticipating Future Legal Trends and Disruptions

Anticipating future legal trends and disruptions is an important component for next-generation legal teams to stay ahead of the curve. The legal landscape is constantly evolving, and it can be difficult to anticipate future trends and disruptions. However, there are a few areas that are likely to see significant changes in the coming years. Here are some key considerations:

- **The Rise of Artificial Intelligence (AI):** AI is already having a major impact on the legal industry, and this trend is only going to accelerate. AI-powered tools are being used to automate tasks, such as legal research and document review. They are also being used to develop new legal products and services. These technologies can significantly impact various legal processes, from contract review to research and data analysis. Familiarity with these technologies can help legal teams streamline their work and provide more efficient services.

- **Ethics and AI:** The use of AI and automation in legal processes can raise ethical questions, such as bias in algorithms or the role of AI in decision-making. Legal teams should consider the ethical implications of AI in the legal field and be prepared to address them in their practice.

- **Contract Management and Risk Mitigation:** With the complexity of business relationships and contracts, corporate counsel must ensure that contracts are well drafted, negotiated, and managed. They need to identify and mitigate contractual risks to protect the company's interests and avoid potential disputes.

- **The Growth of the Gig Economy:** The gig economy is characterized by the rise of short-term, contract-based work. This trend is creating new legal challenges, as it is not always clear who is responsible for the legal rights and obligations of gig workers. The law is also struggling to keep up with the changing nature of work in the gig economy.

- **The Increasing Importance of Data Privacy and Cybersecurity:** With increasing concerns about data privacy and cybersecurity, legal teams need to stay updated on evolving regulations and best practices. New laws or regulations related to data protection can have a significant impact on how organizations collect, store, and process data. Legal teams must proactively adapt to these changes to ensure compliance and protect sensitive information.

- **The Globalization of the Legal Industry:** The legal industry is becoming increasingly globalized as businesses and individuals operate across borders. This trend is creating new challenges for lawyers, who need to be familiar with the laws of multiple jurisdictions. It is also creating new opportunities for lawyers who can help businesses and individuals navigate the complexities of cross-border transactions, such as international trade agreements, data sharing across jurisdictions, and differing regulations in various countries. Staying informed about international law and treaties will be crucial.

- **Remote Work and Virtual Collaboration:** The COVID-19 pandemic of 2020 accelerated the adoption of remote work and virtual collaboration tools. Legal teams should anticipate how these changes might impact legal proceedings, court appearances, and the overall nature of legal practice. Understanding the legal implications of remote work, such as electronic signatures and virtual court proceedings, as well as staying up to date on the various virtual meeting platforms will be essential.

- **Environmental, Social, and Governance (ESG) Issues:** There is a growing emphasis on ESG considerations in business operations. Legal teams will need to understand the legal implications of sustainability, social responsibility, and corporate governance. Legal teams should anticipate shifts in environmental laws and regulations and be prepared to advise organizations on compliance and sustainability initiatives.

- **Healthcare and Biotechnology:** The healthcare and biotechnology sectors are rapidly evolving, with legal implications related to medical advancements, bioethics, and intellectual property. Legal teams should be aware of regulatory changes in these areas and their potential impact on clients or organizations.

- **Alternative Dispute Resolution:** Traditional litigation can be time-consuming and expensive. Anticipating a trend towards alternative dispute resolution methods like arbitration and mediation can help legal teams offer clients more cost-effective and efficient options for resolving conflicts.

- **The Increasing Focus on Social Justice:** Lawyers are increasingly being called upon to use their skills to advance social change. Diversity, equity, and inclusion (DEI) have received increasing attention in the workplace and society at large. Legal teams should be prepared to address legal issues related to discrimination and harassment in the workplace.

- **Political and Geopolitical Changes:** Shifts in political landscapes and geopolitical dynamics can lead to changes in regulations, trade policies, and international relationships. Legal teams should monitor these changes and advise organizations on potential legal impacts.

To effectively anticipate future trends and disruptions, next-generation legal teams should engage in ongoing research, attend relevant conferences and seminars, participate in professional networks, and foster a culture of adaptability within the team. Collaboration with other departments, such as Information Technology (IT), Compliance, and Risk

Management, can also enhance the legal team's ability to stay ahead of emerging challenges.

These are just a few of the legal trends and disruptions that are likely to shape the future of the law and next-generation legal teams.

The Rise of Progressivism Can Bring Challenges to Next-Generation Legal Teams

Progressivism is a political and social philosophy movement that promotes the idea that it's possible to improve society through more robust government intervention and control. Progressivism advocates that the existing constitutional system is outdated and must become an instrument of social change aided by an administrative bureaucracy.

Progressivism promotes the idea that its leaders alone represent "the people" in their struggle; therefore, it is of no great importance whether or not government begins in consent as long as it serves its proper end of transforming society. Democracy and consent are not absolutely rejected by progressives, but their importance is greatly diminished.

Progressives typically define "the people" based on their socioeconomic class, ethnicity, or nationality as they drive their political agenda via political, economic, cultural, and media establishment, supporting their own ideology over the priorities of the masses. The authors of the US Constitution recognized the separation between church and state and the freedom to worship, whereas progressives tend to view the state as divine. Progressives' spiritual development of its citizens may come not through the promotion of religious freedoms but through ideologies such as "saving the planet."

The basic characteristics of progressivism are often found in ideologies, such as liberalism, or socialism, and is not a new phenomenon. The term has been used in several ways, but primarily refers to the Progressive Movement of the late 19th and early 20th centuries. Today, the rise of social media has propelled the progressive movement into the 21st century.

The surge of progressivism could lead to changes in the way laws are made and enforced. Progressive political leaders often appeal to the emotions of the masses, using fear and anger to stoke support for their policies. They may also demonize select groups or ideologies, which can lead to discriminatory laws and practices. Progressivism's impact on next-generation legal teams can be profound and multifaceted.

Challenges Progressivism Can Bring to Next-Generation Legal Teams

- **Shift in Policy Priorities:** Progressive movements often focus on issues that resonate with their political base, which might differ from the priorities of the masses. This could lead to changes in the legislative agenda or regulatory overreach that can lead to excessive bureaucracy and red tape that next-generation legal teams will have to navigate or challenge to succeed.

- **Ambiguity in Legislation:** Progressive political leaders engage in supporting legislation with double meanings that create confusion, ambiguity, and potential misuse. What sounds fair, such as "the new law is aligned with the government's vision for progress and sustainability," is undefined, lacks clarity and could result in advancing particular agendas or arbitrary decisions. Bureaucratic complexity is the tool of progressive political leaders.

- **Threats to Human Rights:** Progressive governments may be less committed to upholding human rights standards, including civil liberties, freedom of speech, freedom of the press, and other personal freedoms and civil liberties. Next-generation legal teams may find themselves at odds with government policies that infringe upon these rights. Defending human rights and civil liberties should be a core mission for legal teams, even in the face of government opposition.

- **Stance on Immigration and Borders:** Progressive agendas often challenge how national border security measures and immigration policies are enforced. The question of whether to change existing immigration laws or not to enforce them is a multifaceted issue that involves various political, economic, social, and ethical considerations. Next-generation legal teams will be faced with the public sentiment of either enforcing existing immigration laws or demanding that Congress find a balance in changing the laws in line with public sentiment. Media coverage plays a significant role in shaping national sentiment and the perceived demonization of either side on this topic.

- **Challenges to International Agreements:** Progressive movements might challenge or renegotiate international agreements and treaties that they perceive as not serving their political interests. This could lead to changes in how international laws and agreements are upheld and enforced.

- **Erosion of Checks and Balances:** Progressive political leaders might attempt to consolidate power by weakening checks and balances, which could impact the separation of powers between the legislative, executive, and judicial branches. This could potentially lead to changes in how laws are made and enforced. Next-generation legal teams will need to defend the rule of law and uphold the principles of justice and fairness even in the face of political pressure.

- **Lack of Accountability:** As the government expands its role in various sectors, there can be a lack of accountability and transparency in the administration of public programs. Next-generation legal teams should advocate for strong oversight mechanisms to ensure that government agencies are accountable for their actions and expenditures.

- **Polarization and Divisiveness:** Progressive movements often thrive on polarizing issues and rhetoric, which can make it difficult for next-generation legal teams to navigate a politically charged environment. They may face increased pressure to take sides in contentious legal cases, potentially compromising their commitment to impartiality and the pursuit of justice.

- **Selective Law Enforcement:** Progressive political leaders might prioritize the enforcement of laws that align with their political agenda, which can include a form of non-enforcement of criminal statutes under the label of "criminal justice reform" while downplaying or neglecting the areas most affected by crime. This could lead to uneven enforcement of existing laws. Next-generation legal teams will need to analyze and respond to these changes, potentially challenging the selective enforcement of laws or the application of unconstitutional laws.

- **Media Influence and Perception of Law:** Progressive political leaders often have strong relationships with media that support their agenda. This can influence public perception of laws, law enforcement, and the justice system.

- **Changes in Constitutional Frameworks:** Progressive political leaders often demand changes to a country's constitutional framework to support their political agenda, altering the fundamental principles that guide lawmaking and enforcement, which may not benefit the masses.

- **Increased Legal Challenges:** Progressive governments and movements often face legal challenges and lawsuits from opposition groups and civil society organizations. Next-generation legal teams may find themselves involved in complex litigation, requiring strategic thinking and advocacy skills.

- **Ethical Dilemmas:** Progressive agendas may present ethical dilemmas for next-generation legal teams. They may need to decide whether to work for or against progressive governments, and these decisions may have long-lasting consequences for their careers and reputations.

The impact of progressivism on the law will vary depending on the specific policies of the progressive political leader in power, whose policies may result in consequences that extend far beyond the immediate political movement.

The rise of progressivism presents significant challenges for next-generation legal teams, but also underscores the crucial role that the legal community plays in safeguarding democracy, human rights, and the rule of law. Next-generation legal teams will be at the forefront of defending these principles in an increasingly complex and polarized world.

Key Challenges Faced by Next–Generation Legal Teams in a Dynamic Business Environment

In a dynamic business environment, next-generation legal teams (in-house and external legal counsel) will face a rapidly evolving business environment that presents both new opportunities and challenges that require them to adapt and evolve their strategies.

To address these challenges, next-generation legal teams will need to be adaptable, tech-savvy, and open to new approaches in legal practice. By embracing these challenges and finding innovative solutions, legal teams will play a vital role in balancing legal risks with business strategies, shaping the future of commerce.

Potential Legal Challenges That Could Be Posed by New Technologies

- **Liability for Harm Caused by Autonomous Systems:** As autonomous systems, such as self-driving cars, become more common, there is a growing risk of harm to people and property. There are many potential parties who may be liable for AI harm—the software developer/provider, algorithm developer, owner, user, network provider, manufacturer, distributor, or other parties involved in the AI application.

- **Intellectual Property Protection for New Technologies:** New technologies, such as artificial intelligence, may be difficult to protect under existing intellectual property laws. This could lead to increased infringement and theft of intellectual property.

- **Privacy Concerns:** New technologies, such as big data and facial recognition, could pose a threat to privacy. It is important to develop laws and regulations that protect people's privacy rights in the digital age.

- **Regulatory Challenges:** New technologies may fall outside the scope of existing laws and regulations. This could create a regulatory vacuum that could be exploited by bad actors. It is important to pursue the development of new laws and regulations that address the specific challenges posed by new technologies.

The legal challenges posed by new technologies are complex and evolving. It is important for lawyers, policymakers, and the public to be aware of these challenges and to work together to develop solutions.

Centers of Excellence for Legal Specialization for Business

The concept of Centers of Excellence (CoE) in the legal field has gained prominence as businesses and industries seek specialized legal expertise to navigate complex regulatory environments and industry-specific challenges. A CoE is typically a team or a group of professionals within a law firm, legal department, or legal consultancy that focuses on a specific legal specialization relevant to a particular business or industry. CoEs offer specialized legal services, research, training, and strategic advice to address the unique legal needs of businesses operating in that sector.

Advantages of Centers of Excellence:

- **In-Depth Knowledge:** CoEs are staffed with legal experts who possess a deep understanding of the specific laws, regulations, and challenges within a particular industry.

- **Tailored Solutions:** CoEs provide customized legal solutions that are aligned with an industry's unique needs and requirements.

- **Risk Mitigation:** By understanding industry-specific risks, CoEs can help businesses mitigate legal risks and navigate compliance challenges effectively.

- **Efficiency:** CoEs streamline processes by centralizing expertise, resulting in quicker and more accurate legal advice.

- **Innovation:** CoEs often lead the development of innovative legal strategies and approaches tailored to an industry's evolving landscape.

- **Thought Leadership:** CoEs can establish thought leadership by producing research, publications, and insights relevant to the industry.

Examples of Industry-Specific Centers of Excellence:

- **Healthcare:** CoEs specializing in healthcare law focus on regulatory compliance, data privacy, medical malpractice, and healthcare litigation.

- **Technology and Intellectual Property (IP):** These CoEs handle IP protection, patent disputes, software licensing, data privacy, and technology transactions.

- **Energy and Environmental:** CoEs in this field address energy regulations, environmental compliance, renewable energy projects, and emissions trading.

- **Financial Services:** CoEs for financial institutions manage regulatory compliance, financial transactions, securities law, and FinTech innovation.

- **Real Estate:** Specialized CoEs in real estate law handle property transactions, land use, zoning, and real estate litigation.

- **Entertainment and Media:** These CoEs manage contracts, copyright issues, media licensing, entertainment contracts, and intellectual property matters in the industry.

Factors Driving Growth of CoEs:

- **Complex Regulations:** Industries often face intricate regulatory frameworks that necessitate specialized legal understanding.

- **Rapid Industry Changes:** Evolving industries require legal teams that can keep up with new trends and technologies.

- **Risk Management:** Growing awareness of legal risks in various sectors has increased the demand for specialized expertise.

- **Litigation Complexity:** Industries prone to disputes benefit from legal teams experienced in handling their unique challenges.

Steps in Establishing CoEs:

- **Identify Need:** Recognize the industry or specialization that requires specialized legal attention.

- **Assemble Experts:** Recruit or allocate legal experts with experience in that field.

- **Knowledge Sharing:** Establish processes for continuous learning, training, and sharing industry insights.

- **Resource Allocation:** Allocate resources for research, technology, and tools specific to the industry.

- **Client Engagement:** Engage with clients to understand their specific needs and challenges.

- **Collaboration:** Foster collaboration between the CoE and other legal teams to provide holistic support.

- **Measuring Performance:** As with any successful endeavor, the CoE must develop the ability to track, measure, and report on the performance of the team's initiatives across all areas of its efforts, as well as specific metrics within the organization itself. This is critical to the growth and evolution of the CoE since clearly demonstrating success will be a major factor in buy-in and support from stakeholders throughout the organization, particularly upper management. All measuring relies on having an established baseline against which to compare performance. At the start of an initiative, the CoE team must immediately identify and establish baselines for the work efforts being performed. These baselines can be developed from internal organizational experiences, industry-accepted and published standards, or both.

The growth of CoEs for specific legal specializations in various industries reflects the increasing need for tailored legal services. CoEs offer industry-specific expertise, facilitate compliance, and contribute to the overall success of businesses in their respective sectors. As industries continue to evolve, the demand for these specialized legal services is positioned to grow.

Next-generation legal teams (in-house and external legal counsel) will face a rapidly evolving business environment that presents both new opportunities and challenges that require them to adapt and evolve their strategies.

Although the role of corporate legal counsel is evolving in response to emerging trends, next-generation legal teams must still adhere to core responsibilities which remain the same: to provide strategic legal advice, manage legal risk, resolve disputes, encourage higher standards of ethics and compliance, and help businesses succeed in the future business landscape.

Epilogue

The delicate balance between legal risks and business strategies continues to evolve, reflecting the ever-changing landscape of commerce and regulation. As industries push the boundaries of innovation, the need for a harmonious coexistence between legal compliance and entrepreneurial ambition becomes increasingly apparent.

Forward-thinking business leaders recognize that collaboration between legal experts and business strategists can be the cornerstone of success. Legal teams should no longer be seen as mere gatekeepers but as integral partners in shaping the contours of new ventures. The legal team, whether in-house or external, can help guide the development of business strategies that not only capitalize on market trends but also navigate the intricacies of legal risks and regulatory frameworks.

As the bold but cautious journey continues to unfold, one thing remains clear: the balance between legal risks and business strategies is a fluid and dynamic relationship. It thrives on adaptability, transparency, and a willingness to learn from the past. In this era of unprecedented connectivity and innovation, the story of balancing legal risks with business strategies serves as a testament to the power of collaboration, foresight, and a shared commitment to shaping a future where commerce and compliance walk hand in hand.

The author's books, *Chasing Corporate Compliance* and *Bold But Cautious* share a strong connection through the concepts of corporate compliance and legal frameworks and their

application in the contexts of business strategy and operations. *Chasing Corporate Compliance* focuses on building and
implementing a compliance program through the principles
and practical application of regulatory compliance. *Bold But
Cautious* delves deeper into the legal risks and mitigation strategies essential for business innovation and achievement. Both
emphasize the significance of understanding and adhering to
the legal requirements and ethical standards in the business
world.

GLOSSARY OF TERMS

Alternative Dispute Resolution (ADR): Alternative dispute resolution (ADR) is a process in which a neutral third party—a mediator or arbitrator—helps parties who are embroiled in a dispute come to an agreement as an alternative to litigation.

Anti-Money Laundering (AML): Anti-money laundering (AML) refers to the regulations and procedures designed to prevent, identify, and uncover efforts to disguise illicit funds as legitimate income.

Antitrust Law: Regulations that encourage competition by limiting the market power of a particular firm. This often involves ensuring that mergers and acquisitions do not overtly concentrate large market power or form monopolies. In the United States, antitrust law is a collection of mostly federal laws that regulate the conduct and organization of businesses to promote competition and prevent unjustified monopolies. The three main US antitrust statutes are the Sherman Act of 1890, the Clayton Act of 1914, and the Federal Trade Commission Act of 1914.

Bank Secrecy Act (BSA): The Bank Secrecy Act is a US law requiring financial institutions in the United States to assist US government agencies in detecting and preventing money laundering.

Bid-Rigging: Bid rigging occurs when a group of bidders unlawfully band together and conspire with one another to devise strategies to reduce competition in a bidding process and determine the bid winner.

Bitcoin: Bitcoin is a cryptocurrency, which is a digital currency designed to act as money in peer-to-peer transactions outside the control of a third-party financial institution.

Blockchain: A secure and decentralized online record of transactions that have been made in cryptocurrency and maintained across several computers linked in a peer-to-peer network. Blockchains can also be used to make data in any industry immutable—the term used to describe the inability to be altered, which offers the possibility of creating a fraud-proof system for transacting exchanges.

Bold: Showing an ability to take risks; confident and courageous.

Buy-In: When employees accept strategy, decisions or changes and engage in a commitment to working together with respect to individuals, teams, departments, etc.

California Consumer Privacy Act (CCPA) The CCPA grants California consumers certain rights regarding their personal information and requires businesses meeting certain criteria to be transparent about data collection and sharing practices. In addition to other consumer protection requirements, there are thresholds to fall within the statute's scope to be subject to this law.

Cautious: The exercise of careful consideration of what will be necessary to avoid potential problems or dangers.

Center of Excellence (CoE): A Center of Excellence in the law practice sense is a team or a group of professionals within a law firm, legal department, or legal consultancy that focuses on a specific legal specialization relevant to a particular business or industry.

Checks and Balances: Checks and balances are applied in constitutional governments, where there is a separation and sharing of powers among the different branches of government, legislative, executive, and judicial branches, giving adequate power to the different branches to check the powers of other branches.

Colorado Privacy Act (CPA): The CPA grants Colorado consumers rights with respect to their personal data, including the right to access, delete, and correct their personal data, as well as the right to opt out of the sale of their personal data or its use for targeted advertising or certain kinds of profiling. In addition to other consumer protection requirements, there are thresholds to fall within the statute's scope to be subject to this law.

Comparative Advertising: Comparative advertising is a marketing strategy in which a company's product or service is presented as superior when compared to a competitor's.

Connecticut Data Privacy Act (CTDPA): The CTDPA contains many similarities to the existing peer legislation in California, Virginia, and Colorado, but it also possesses its own unique differences. In addition to other consumer protection requirements, there are thresholds to fall within the statute's scope to be subject to this law.

Consumer Financial Protection Bureau (CFPB): Agency of the federal government created to provide a single point of accountability for enforcing federal financial consumer protection laws.

Convertible Virtual Currency (CVC): A digital asset that has an equivalent value in real currency or acts as a substitute for real currency. A cryptocurrency is an example of a convertible virtual currency that can be used as payment for goods and services, digitally traded between users, and exchanged for or into real currencies or digital assets.

Cryptocurrency: Any form of currency that only exists digitally, that usually has no central issuing or regulating authority but instead uses a decentralized system to record transactions and manage the issuance of new units, and that relies on cryptography to prevent counterfeiting and fraudulent transactions.

Cryptography: The technique of securing information and communications through the use of codes, i.e., mathematical concepts and a set of rule-based calculations called algorithms, to transform messages so that only the person for whom the information is intended can understand and process it.

Cyber Attack: A malicious and deliberate attempt by an individual or organization to breach the information system of another individual or organization. Usually, the attacker seeks some type of benefit from disrupting the victim's network.

Cyber Incident Reporting for Critical Infrastructure Act of 2022 (CIRCIA): The CIRCIA is nestled within the Consolidated Appropriations Act of 2022 and requires companies operating in critical infrastructure sectors to report covered cyber incidents within 72 hours of the companies' reasonable belief that a cyber incident has occurred and report ransom payments within 24 hours after payment is made.

Cybersecurity: Measures taken to protect a computer or computer system against unauthorized access or attack.

Data Breach: Any security incident in which unauthorized parties gain access to sensitive data or confidential information.

Data Protection Authorities (DPAs): Independent organizations that uphold data protection rights across their territory.

Data Security: Data security restricts access to data and protects data from compromise by external attackers and malicious insiders.

Digital Payments: The transfer of value from one payment account to another using a digital device such as a mobile phone or computer, also called an electronic payment (e-payment), with no exchange of actual cash being involved.

Diversity, Equity, and Inclusion (DEI): Refers to an organization's culture and operational frameworks intended to promote the fair and equitable treatment of people, particularly groups who have historically been underrepresented or subject to discrimination.

Environmental, Social, and Governance (ESG): A framework that helps investors, employees, customers and others understand how an organization is managing risks and opportunities related to environmental, social, and governance criteria.

Equal Credit Opportunity Act (ECOA): Makes it unlawful for any creditor to discriminate against any applicant with respect to any aspect of a credit transaction.

Ethereum: A blockchain-based platform with smart contract functionality best known for its cryptocurrency, ether (ETH).

External Legal Counsel (also known as Outside Counsel): Legal counsel retained from an external law firm to provide legal services to an organization.

Federal Information Security Management Act: Defines a framework for managing information security that must be followed for all information systems used or operated by a US federal government agency in the executive or legislative branches or by a contractor or other organization on behalf of a federal agency in those branches.

Federal Trade Commission (FTC): Agency of the federal government that administers consumer protection legislation against unfair, deceptive or fraudulent practices in the marketplace.

Federal Trade Commission Act: The Federal Trade Commission Act of 1914 is a United States federal law that established the Federal Trade Commission.

FinTech: Refers to financial technology that seeks to improve and automate the delivery and use of financial services. Artificial intelligence, blockchain, cloud computing, and big data are regarded as the four key areas of FinTech. The use of smartphones for mobile banking, investing, borrowing, and cryptocurrency are examples.

Force Majeure: In contract law, *force majeure* (from French "overwhelming force, superior force") is a common clause in contracts that essentially frees both parties from liability or obligation when an extraordinary event or circumstance beyond the control of the parties, such as a war, strike, riot, crime, epidemic, or sudden legal change prevents one or both parties from fulfilling their obligations under the contract.

Foreign Corrupt Practices Act (FCPA): A United States anti-corruption law that prohibits US firms and individuals from paying bribes to foreign officials to assist in obtaining or retaining business.

General Data Protection Regulation (GDPR): A legal framework that sets guidelines and imposes obligations onto organizations anywhere when they collect and process the personal information of individuals who live in the European Union (EU).

Geopolitical: Relating to or concerning the influence of such factors as geography, economics, and demography on politics, especially in international relations.

Gig Economy: The term is borrowed from the music world, where performers book "gigs" that are single or short-term engagements at various venues. The gig economy is based on flexible, temporary, or short-term contract or freelance jobs, as opposed to permanent jobs:

Globalization: A term used to describe the increasing connectedness and interdependence of world cultures and economies, where social and cultural influences gradually become similar in all parts of the world.

Gramm-Leach-Bliley Act (GLBA): Requires financial institutions— companies that offer consumers financial products or services like loans, financial or investment advice, or insurance – to explain their information-sharing practices to their customers and to ensure the security and confidentiality of nonpublic, personal information of customer records.

Health Insurance Portability and Accountability Act (HIPAA): Applies to healthcare organizations in the United States and sets standards for the security and privacy of patients' medical records and other health-related information.

Howey Test: A set of standards that an investment must meet for the Securities and Exchange Commission (SEC) to consider it a security and regulate it as such. It derives its name from a 1946 US Supreme Court case called "SEC v. W.J. Howey Co." (SEC v. W. J. Howey Co., 328 US 293, 66 S. Ct. 1100, 90 L. Ed.

1244, 163 A.L.R. 1043, May 27, 1946), which set the precedent for how securities laws should be applied to certain investment arrangements.

Impact: In risk management, an estimate of the potential losses associated with an identified risk.

In-House Legal Counsel: A lawyer or team of lawyers that works within a corporation instead of within a law firm and handles the legal needs of the company for whom they work.

Initial Coin Offering (ICO): A term for the initial release of a new digital asset. Initial coin offers typically start with a new or established company that's looking to raise capital for growth. For practical purposes, you can think of a digital coin as equivalent to a share of stock. When a business has an ICO, it sells coins for dollars. The new currency should theoretically follow the value of the company or underlying service. That's why the SEC often treats ICOs similar to other securities offerings and requires compliance with its laws.

Insiders: A term describing a director or senior officer of a publicly traded company, as well as any person or entity that beneficially owns more than 10% of a company's voting shares. For purposes of insider trading, the definition is expanded to include anyone who trades a company's shares based on material nonpublic knowledge.

InsurTech: Refers to the use of technology innovations designed to find cost savings and efficiency from the current insurance industry model. InsurTech is a combination of the words "insurance" and "technology," inspired by the term FinTech.

Intellectual Property (IP): A work or invention that is the result of creativity, such as literary and artistic works; designs;

logos and symbols; and names and images used in commerce for which one may apply for a patent, copyright, trademark, etc.

Key Risk Indicator (KRI): An indicator or metric used to assess and measure a possible risk. KRIs can provide advance notice of potential risks or insight into possible weaknesses in an organization's operations.

Know Your Customer (KYC): KYC is part of financial institutions legally required due diligence to verify the identity of customers and monitor their transactions to detect suspicious activity and prevent criminals and terrorists from moving money through the financial system.

Legal Precedent: Refers to a court decision that is considered as authority for deciding subsequent cases involving identical or similar facts or similar legal issues. Precedent is incorporated into the doctrine of stare decisis and requires courts to apply the law in the same manner to cases with the same facts. Stare decisis is the doctrine that courts will adhere to precedent in making their decisions. Stare decisis means "to stand by things decided" in Latin.

Legal Risk Tolerance: Refers to an organization's willingness and capacity to accept, tolerate, and manage various degrees of risk in pursuit of their business objectives and goals.

LegalTech: Refers to the use of technology and software to provide legal services and support the legal industry. It can encompass tools and software that assist with legal research, contract management, electronic discovery, document automation, and virtual law firms. LegalTech is a combination of the words "legal" and "technology," inspired by the term FinTech.

Likelihood: A qualitative assessment that is subjective and refers to the possibility that a particular outcome will happen.

Macro Trends: A long-term directional shift that affects a large population, often on a global scale. For example, climate change, urbanization, changing demographics.

MedTech: The application of technology to healthcare and medicine. This can include devices, software, and processes that enhance patient care, diagnosis, treatment, and research.

Neobanks: Digital-only banks that don't have any physical branches.

NIST Cybersecurity Framework: A set of guidelines for mitigating organizational cybersecurity risks, published by the US National Institute of Standards and Technology (NIST).

OECD Anti-Bribery Convention: The Council of the Organization for Economic Co-operation and Development (OECD) is an anti-bribery convention that is a legally binding international agreement combating bribery of foreign public officials in international business and requires signatory countries to criminalize bribery of foreign public officials.

Office of Foreign Assets Control (OFAC): The Office of Foreign Assets Control (OFAC) of the US Department of the Treasury administers and enforces economic and trade sanctions based on US foreign policy against targeted foreign countries and regimes, terrorists, international narcotics traffickers, those engaged in weapons of mass destruction, and other threats to national security.

Payment Card Industry Data Security Standard (PCI DSS): A widely accepted set of policies and procedures intended to optimize the security of credit, debit and cash card transactions and protect cardholders against misuse of their personal information.

Pilot Programs: A feasibility study or experimental trial that is a small-scale, short-term experiment that helps an organization learn how a large-scale project might work in practice.

Price-Fixing: An agreement (written, verbal, or inferred from conduct) among competitors to raise, lower, maintain, or stabilize prices or price levels. Antitrust laws require that each company establish prices and other competitive terms on its own without agreeing with a competitor. Individuals and companies that knowingly enter price-fixing agreements are routinely investigated by the FBI and other federal law enforcement agencies and can be criminally prosecuted.

Privacy Act: The Privacy Act of 1974, as amended, 5 U.S.C. § 552a, establishes a code of fair information practices that governs the collection, maintenance, use, and dissemination of information about individuals that is maintained in systems of records by federal agencies.

Product Liability: The area of law in which manufacturers, distributors, suppliers, retailers, and others who make products available to the public are held responsible for the injuries those products cause.

Progressivism: A social or political movement that holds that it is possible to improve human societies through political change and the support of government actions.

Prudence: Care, caution, and good judgment, as well as wisdom in looking ahead.

Qualitative: Assessment that is subjective and describes qualities or characteristics rather than numeric quantities.

Quantitative: Assessment that is numeric and can be measured and shown in numbers and amounts.

Risk Mitigation: A strategy to prepare for and lessen the effects of threats faced by a business.

Risk Prioritization: The process of identifying the most critical risks so they can be addressed first. Priorities should be set using the likelihood of a risk and the potential impact it poses to the company.

Risk Ranking: The risk level expressed as low, moderate or high, based on the impact and likelihood ranking of the risk. The risk level provides the basis for prioritization and action.

Securities Act of 1933: The Securities Act of 1933 was created and passed into law to protect investors after the stock market crash of 1929. The legislation had two main goals: to ensure more transparency in financial statements so investors could make informed decisions about investments and to establish laws against misrepresentation and fraudulent activities in the securities markets.

Security Token Offerings (STOs): A type of public offering in which tokenized digital securities are sold in security token exchanges. Tokens can be used to trade real financial assets and are stored and validated in a blockchain virtual ledger system.

Smart Contracts: A computer program or transaction protocol that is intended to automatically execute, control, or document events and actions according to the terms of a contract.

Stakeholder: An individual, group or organization that's impacted by the outcome of a project or a business venture. Stakeholders have an interest in the success of the project and can be investors, employees, customers, and suppliers.

Tort: An act or omission that gives rise to injury or harm to another or their property and amounts to a civil wrong for which courts impose liability in the form of damages.

Truth in Lending Act (TILA): Requires lenders to disclose their terms and costs to consumers in a standardized manner so that consumers can shop and compare loans.

UK Bribery Act: The United Kingdom Bribery Act 2010 is the primary anti-corruption law in the United Kingdom that punishes public and private bribery. The UK Bribery Act covers UK citizens, residents and organizations that originate from the UK or conduct business in the country.

UK Investigatory Powers Act 2016: Act of the Parliament of the United Kingdom regulating the powers of public bodies to carry out surveillance and investigation and covering the interception of communications.

United Nations Convention against Corruption: The only legally binding international anti-corruption multilateral treaty adopted by member states of the United Nations in October 2003 and entered into force in December 2005. The treaty recognizes the importance of both preventive and punitive measures and addresses the cross-border nature of corruption with provisions on international cooperation and on the return of the proceeds of corruption.

United Nations Convention on Contracts for the International Sale of Goods (CISG): The CISG provides a uniform and fair regime for contracts for the international sale of goods between private businesses, excluding sales to consumers, as well as sales of certain specified types of goods, for purposes of introducing certainty in commercial exchanges and decreasing transaction costs. It applies to contracts for the sales of goods between parties whose places of business are in different Contracting States or may also apply by virtue of the parties' choice.

US Securities and Exchange Commission (SEC): Agency of the federal government that regulates securities markets and protects investors.

USA PATRIOT Act: Legislation passed in 2001 to improve the abilities of US law enforcement to detect and deter terrorism. The act's official title is "Uniting and Strengthening America by Providing Appropriate Tools Required to Intercept and Obstruct Terrorism."

Utah Consumer Privacy Act (UCPA): The UCPA borrows many core elements from peer legislation in California, Virginia, and Colorado but also possesses its own unique differences, thus adding to the growing patchwork of state privacy laws that have been forming absent a federal rule. There are thresholds to fall within the statute's scope to be subject to this law.

Utility Token: a digital token of cryptocurrency that is sold as a method of fundraising for the issuing start-up and that can later be used to purchase goods or services offered by the issuer of the cryptocurrency.

Vendor Legal Risk Management: The process of ensuring that the use of third-party service providers does not create a potential for legal liability, regulatory violations, business disruption, financial and reputational damage or a negative impact on business performance.

Veterans Affairs Information Security Act: A Veterans Health Administration (VHA) directive that establishes technical and physical safeguards to ensure the security and confidentiality of records that contain VHA personally identifiable information (PII) and personal health information (PHI) in the Department of Veterans Affairs (VA) Information Technology (IT) systems in operation within VHA business lines.

Virginia Consumer Data Protection Act (VCDPA): The VCDPA gives Virginia consumers the right to access their personal data and request that it be deleted by businesses. It also requires companies to conduct data protection assessments related to processing personal data for targeted advertising and sales purposes. In addition to other consumer protection requirements, there are thresholds to fall within the statute's scope to be subject to this law.

RESOURCES

The following resources are offered as a pathway to additional information for the reader to explore in delving deeper into the subject matter.

Airbnb, Inc. Annual Report Form 10-K For the Fiscal Year Ended December 31, 2022

Airbnb, Inc. Annual Report Form 10-K For the Fiscal Year Ended December 31, 2021

Airbnb, Inc. Annual Report Form 10-K For the Fiscal Year Ended December 31, 2020

Alphabet Inc. Annual Report Form 10-K For the Fiscal Year Ended December 31, 2022

Alphabet Inc. Annual Report Form 10-K For the Fiscal Year Ended December 31, 2021

Alphabet Inc. Annual Report Form 10-K For the Fiscal Year Ended December 31, 2020

Alphabet Inc. Annual Report Form 10-K For the Fiscal Year Ended December 31, 2019

Alphabet Inc. Annual Report Form 10-K For the Fiscal Year Ended December 31, 2018

Amazon Annual Report Form 10-K For the Fiscal Year Ended December 31, 2022

Amazon Annual Report Form 10-K For the Fiscal Year Ended December 31, 2021

Amazon Annual Report Form 10-K For the Fiscal Year Ended December 31, 2020

Amazon Annual Report Form 10-K For the Fiscal Year Ended December 31, 2019

Amazon Annual Report Form 10-K For the Fiscal Year Ended December 31, 2018

Apple Annual Report Form 10-K For the Fiscal Year Ended September 30, 2023

Apple Annual Report Form 10-K For the Fiscal Year Ended September 24, 2022

Apple Annual Report Form 10-K For the Fiscal Year Ended September 25, 2021

Apple Annual Report Form 10-K For the Fiscal Year Ended September 26, 2020

Apple Annual Report Form 10-K For the Fiscal Year Ended September 28, 2019

Apple Annual Report Form 10-K For the Fiscal Year Ended September 29, 2018

Apple Annual Report Form 10-K For the Fiscal Year Ended September 30, 2017

Bank Secrecy Act (BSA)

California Consumer Privacy Act (CCPA)

Colorado Privacy Act (CPA)

Connecticut Data Privacy Act (CTDPA)

Consumer Financial Protection Bureau (CFPB)

Cyber Incident Reporting for Critical Infrastructure Act of 2022 (CIRCIA)

Equal Employment Opportunity Commission (EEOC)

Facebook, Inc. Annual Report Form 10-K For the Fiscal Year Ended December 31, 2020

Facebook, Inc. Annual Report Form 10-K For the Fiscal Year Ended December 31, 2019

Facebook, Inc. Annual Report Form 10-K For the Fiscal Year Ended December 31, 2018

Facebook, Inc. Annual Report Form 10-K For the Fiscal Year Ended December 31, 2017

Fair Credit Reporting Act (FCRA)

Federal Deposit Insurance Corporation (FDIC)

Federal Trade Commission (FTC)

Financial Crimes and Enforcement Network (FinCEN)

Foreign Corrupt Practices Act (FCPA)

General Data Protection Regulation (GDPR)

Gramm-Leach-Bliley Act (GLBA)

Health Insurance Portability and Accountability Act (HIPAA)

Meta Platforms, Inc. Annual Report Form 10-K For the Fiscal Year Ended December 31, 2022

Meta Platforms, Inc. Annual Report Form 10-K For the Fiscal Year Ended December 31, 2021

Microsoft Annual Report Form 10-K For the Fiscal Year Ended June 30, 2023

Microsoft Annual Report Form 10-K For the Fiscal Year Ended June 20, 2022

Microsoft Annual Report Form 10-K For the Fiscal Year Ended June 30, 2021

Microsoft Annual Report Form 10-K For the Fiscal Year Ended June 20, 2020

Microsoft Annual Report Form 10-K For the Fiscal Year Ended June 30, 2019

Microsoft Annual Report Form 10-K For the Fiscal Year Ended June 30, 2018

Microsoft Annual Report Form 10-K For the Fiscal Year Ended June 30, 2017

Microsoft Annual Report Form 10-K For the Fiscal Year Ended June 30, 2016

Netflix, Inc. Annual Report Form 10-K For the Fiscal Year Ended December 31, 2022

Netflix, Inc. Annual Report Form 10-K For the Fiscal Year Ended December 31, 2021

Netflix, Inc. Annual Report Form 10-K For the Fiscal Year Ended December 31, 2020

Netflix, Inc. Annual Report Form 10-K For the Fiscal Year Ended December 31, 2019

Netflix, Inc. Annual Report Form 10-K For the Fiscal Year Ended December 31, 2018

Netflix, Inc. Annual Report Form 10-K For the Fiscal Year Ended December 31, 2017

NIST Cybersecurity Framework

Occupational Safety and Health Administration (OSHA)

Office of Foreign Assets Control (OFAC)

Privacy Act of 1974

Tesla, Inc. Annual Report Form 10-K For the Fiscal Year Ended
December 31, 2022

Tesla, Inc. Annual Report Form 10-K For the Fiscal Year Ended
December 31, 2021

Tesla, Inc. Annual Report Form 10-K For the Fiscal Year Ended
December 31, 2020

Tesla, Inc. Annual Report Form 10-K For the Fiscal Year Ended
December 31, 2019

Tesla, Inc. Annual Report Form 10-K For the Fiscal Year Ended
December 31, 2018

Uber Technologies, Inc. Annual Report Form 10-K For the
Fiscal Year Ended December 31, 2022

Uber Technologies, Inc. Annual Report Form 10-K For the
Fiscal Year Ended December 31, 2021

Uber Technologies, Inc. Annual Report Form 10-K For the
Fiscal Year Ended December 31, 2020

Uber Technologies, Inc. Annual Report Form 10-K For the
Fiscal Year Ended December 31, 2019

UK Bribery Act 2010

UK Investigatory Powers Act 2016

United Nations Convention against Corruption

United Nations Convention on Contracts for the International
Sale of Goods (CISG)

US Department of Justice (DOJ)

US Securities and Exchange Commission (SEC)

USA PATRIOT Act

Utah Consumer Privacy Act (UCPA)

Veterans Affairs Information Security Act

Virginia Consumer Data Protection Act (VCDPA)

Walmart Inc. Annual Report Form 10-K For the Fiscal Year Ended January 31, 2023

Walmart Inc. Annual Report Form 10-K For the Fiscal Year Ended January 31, 2022

Walmart Inc. Annual Report Form 10-K For the Fiscal Year Ended January 31, 2021

Walmart Inc. Annual Report Form 10-K For the Fiscal Year Ended January 31, 2020

Walmart Inc. Annual Report Form 10-K For the Fiscal Year Ended January 31, 2019

Walmart Inc. Annual Report Form 10-K For the Fiscal Year Ended January 31, 2018

Walmart Inc. Annual Report Form 10-K For the Fiscal Year Ended January 31, 2017

www.ingramcontent.com/pod-product-compliance
Lightning Source LLC
Chambersburg PA
CBHW071504140726
47997CB00005B/1848